The Dark Red Amulet

ORAL INSTRUCTIONS ON THE
PRACTICE OF VAJRAKILAYA

by

Khenchen Palden Sherab Rinpoche

and

Khenpo Tsewang Dongyal Rinpoche

Samye Translation Group

Snow Lion
Boulder

SNOW LION
An imprint of Shambhala Publications, Inc.
2129 13th Street
Boulder, Colorado 80302
www.shambhala.com

Previously published as a commentary by Dharma Samudra in 1992.

14 13 12 11 10 9 8 7 6

Printed in the United States of America

Shambhala Publications makes every effort to print on acid-free, recycled paper.
Snow Lion is distributed worldwide by Penguin Random House, Inc., and its subsidiaries.

Text design by Rita Frizzell, Dakini Graphics

Library of Congress Cataloging-in-Publication Data

Palden Sherab, Khenchen, 1941–
The dark red amulet: oral instructions on the practice of Vajrakilaya /
Khenchen Palden Sherab Rinpoche and Khenpo Tsewang Dongyal Rinpoche.
p. cm.
Includes bibliographical references.
ISBN 978-1-55939-311-9 (alk. paper)
1. Vajrakilaya (Buddhist deity) I. Tsewang Dongyal, Khenpo, 1950– II. Title.
BQ4890.V336P35 2008
294.3'444—dc22
2008020817

As with all Vajrayana practices, Vajrakilaya should not be practiced without receiving an empowerment or reading transmission directly from a qualified lineage master. Please do not attempt to practice these Vajrakilaya instructions without proper authorization and lineage blessings.

Table of Contents

TABLE OF CONTENTS

*Khenchen Palden Sherab Rinpoche (right) and Khenpo Tsewang
Dongyal Rinpoche (left) at Padma Samye Ling*

Preface

This book is a commentary based on a *terma* text discovered by Tsasum Lingpa in the seventeenth century in Tibet. The root text is a sadhana practice combining Yangdak Heruka and Dorje Phurba (Vajrakilaya), a sadhana of "Yang-Phur." From this larger volume, medium, short, and condensed versions have been translated with the help of many of our students. The entire volume is entitled *The Dark Red Amulet of Unsurpassable Yang-Phur*. The short sadhana is "The Coemergent Union of the Vajra Hero," and the condensed sadhana is "The Practice of the HUNG of the Powerful Black Phurba."

The line-by-line commentary in this book follows the short and condensed versions and was compiled from Vajrakilaya teachings given during the early 1990s in Estes Park, Colorado (August 1990), Denver, Colorado (June 1991 and September 1992), the Zuni River Valley, New Mexico (July 1991), and West Palm Beach, Florida (October 1991).

For the sections of the practice text to be chanted aloud, two lines of Tibetan are included with each line of English, of which the second is a transcription of pronunciation that is similar to the Khampa dialect.

This book begins with three introductory prayers. The first supplication, composed by Guru Padmasambhava, is part of the *Northern Terma* discovered by Rigdzin Gödem. The second and third prayers were written in Tibetan by Khenchen Palden Sherab and translated into English by Khenpo Tsewang Dongyal. With regard to the dedication prayers at the end of the book, the first prayer was written by a master of the Kama lineage, the second was written by Lady Yeshe Tsogyal, and the third was spoken by Buddha Shakyamuni in his Mahayana biography, *Lalitavistara*.

We would like to express our gratitude to all our students who translated the sadhanas, transcribed and edited the commentary, and contributed to the completion of this book. Special thanks go to editors Ann Helm, Steve Harris, and Elizabeth Gongde, to Nancy Roberts for coordinating the publication, and to the artists whose work is reproduced herein.

Ven. Khenchen Palden Sherab Rinpoche
Ven. Khenpo Tsewang Dongyal Rinpoche
Palden Padma Samye Ling

Introductory Prayers

The realization of great glorious Vajrakumara
Brought blessing to the spontaneously accomplished and Mahamudra
vidyadharas
And to Padmasambhava Dorje Tötreng Tsal.
I supplicate the lamas of the activity lineage
Of the past, present, and future,
I supplicate Orgyen Padmakara.

The vajra wrath of bodhichitta, of love and compassion—the great skillful
means—will totally cut blazing anger and attachment.
The emptiness vajra of great wisdom, free from complexities, pure from the
beginning, will instantly destroy the darkness and confused vision of
ignorance.
The spontaneously accomplished union of skillful means and wisdom—
vajra and padma—transforms all dualities and characteristics of
samsara and nirvana into the originally liberated three-kaya state.
The all-pervasive lord, the embodiment of the mandala of all buddha
families, is Vajrakumara with his consort, who is none other than one's
own awareness.
To recognize this through undistracted mindfulness is to reveal the reverence
of one's deepest heart.

In the vast secret charnel ground of Akanishta,
Great Vajrakumara, the all-pervasive lord of all buddha families,
Gave the oceanlike hundred thousand teachings of Kilaya.
From that I will joyfully share a festival of reliable essence teachings.

Tsasum Lingpa

Introduction

Tsasum Lingpa was one of the great *tertöns* in the history of the Nyingma School of Tibetan Buddhism. He lived during one of the very crucial times in Tibetan history when there were many disturbances faced by practitioners and much political turmoil in Tibet. Tsasum Lingpa was also one of the leading examples of tertöns who revealed terma teachings from objects and different locations—he discovered many personal ritual objects that belonged to Guru Padmasambhava, Yeshe Tsogyal, and King Trisong Deutsen, and other great yogis and yoginis of the eighth century.

Tsasum Lingpa is renowned as a crazy wisdom tertön. Guru Padmasambhava and Yeshe Tsogyal had predicted, "Suddenly tertöns will manifest and discover termas randomly like clouds in the sky, benefiting others in very targeted ways." Tsasum Lingpa began to reveal terma teachings around the age of eighteen, and continued revealing terma into his early forties.

According to the Great Jamgon Kongtrul, "Tsasum Lingpa's lifespan seems to have been about forty-four years long. After he passed away, his followers maintained and spread his terma teachings well. When he died, he emanated three reincarnations. His body emanation was Rongmyon Orgyen Rigdzin, who presided as head of Trimzig Monastery. His speech emanation, Kunzang Norbu, was born around Gawalung area, but there were no further speech incarnations after him. His mind emanation, Rigdzin Mijig Dorje, was born in the Chungpo area. Both his body and mind incarnations continue up to the present time."

Tsasum Lingpa's teachings were very strongly established in the Doshul region of eastern Tibet. The largest monastery of his lineage is Gochen

Monastery. There are also many other small monasteries where his teachings are practiced and followed, thus keeping Tsasum Lingpa's lineage alive and well. His teachings are also well maintained in the Puwo region of southern Tibet, where Tsasum Lingpa himself founded the Dudul Ngagpa Ling Monastery, and in the Drongpa region of Nangchen.

However, due to the difficult situations and circumstances in Tibet during the twentieth century, the Tsasum Lingpa lineage teachings have nearly disappeared. Many other Tibetan Buddhist lineages have also been shaken. My brother, Venerable Khenchen Palden Sherab Rinpoche, along with my father, Lama Chimed Namgyal, and myself may have been the only people who brought and kept these lineage teachings outside of Tibet until the late 1970s. In the early 1980s the Chinese government's policies in Tibet began to become a little more open, so that other teachers upholding Tsasum Lingpa's lineage, such as Tulku Sang-ngag Rinpoche, were able to leave Tibet and preserve and spread the teachings of Tsasum Lingpa. Currently, in the Chungpo region of Tibet the mind incarnation of Tsasum Lingpa, commonly known as Nanchag Tulku, along with many others, is actively establishing monasteries and spreading these teachings once again in the Chungpo, Doshul, and other regions. Due to the kind efforts of many supporters, Khenchen Palden Sherab and I published these lineage teachings in India, distributing the texts to devotees in India, Tibet, and throughout the Himalayan region. At that time, the Library of Congress included these texts as a part of their Asian collection, distributing them to about twenty universities throughout the United States.

This very short life story of Tsasum Lingpa according to the Great Khyentse has been added to ornament this new publication. The Great Khyentse, who embodies the wisdom, compassion, and activities of all Buddhist masters, was appointed and entrusted by Guru Padmasambhava as his regent to reestablish and restrengthen many lost and weakened Tibetan Buddhist teachings, along with the Great Kongtrul.

At this time we are extremely delighted to be able to publish these teachings of Vajrakilaya, based on the oral instruction lineage according to the termas of Tsasum Lingpa, in English. We hope that many more publications of this great hidden tertön will soon be available. This book on Vajrakilaya is not solely a teaching by Tsasum Lingpa; in our commentary, we are trying to convey the essential meaning of the general and particular Vajrakilaya teachings within the entire scope of all of the nine yanas. Therefore, we hope that this will support all practitioners of Buddhism, and Vajrayana practitioners in particular. May they all discover the absolute vajra nature that will transform every duality hindrance into clear wisdom and compassion.

Venerable Khenpo Tsewang Dongyal Rinpoche
Padma Samye Ling, October 2, 2006

Nub Sangye Yeshe Rinpoche, one of the nine heartlike students of
Guru Padmasambhava and a previous incarnation of Tsasum Lingpa

A Brief Biography of
Great Tertön Tsasum Lingpa

by Jamyang Khyentse Pema Ösel Dongnag Lingpa

The reincarnation of Nubchen Sangye Yeshe known as Tsasum Terdag Lingpa or Garwang Namchag Dorje was born in the eleventh *rabjung*, although the year of his birth is unclear. His father, Tashi, was from Drupchen Ling, and his mother, Gelekma, was from the area known as Ngarong, which is near the slopes of the secret mountains Jowo Zegyal and Kugyal Shan in the Ngachen region of Tibet.

At the time of his birth, numerous amazing signs and visions appeared. When he was very young, he received refuge vows and teachings from Lama Karda Chöje, the head lama of the Karda Monastery of the Gelugpa School, who was known as the reincarnation of Ngog Loden Sherab. Upon receiving these vows, he received the name Tashi Phuntsok and entered the monastery, where he memorized some daily ritual ceremonies and sadhanas.

At a very early age, he received a teaching from the great tertön Tagsham Terchen, who was visiting the town of Ngachen Gar, thus forging a dharma connection between them. No accounts of his life indicate that he contacted or received teachings from any other teachers at this time.

Tsasum Lingpa's behavior was so wild that it was very difficult for him to get along with the other monks. The monastery appointed him as "the collector of donations for the monastery," and when Lama Karda Chöje went to central Tibet to make offerings, Tsasum Lingpa joined him as an attendant. This was during the time of the White Lotus Holder Yeshe Gyamtso and his dharma patron, King Lhazang. Young Tsasum Lingpa was so smart that Lama Chöje encouraged him to study philosophy, but since it had been predicted that he would reveal many profound and timely terma teachings, he did not stay for a long time in central Tibet, but instead returned to Kham.

Subsequently he returned to central Tibet, where he contacted Könchog Thinley Zangpo of Drigung Monastery who became his root teacher. He stayed for about three years in that monastery and received many teachings, particularly the oral pith instruction lineage teachings of the Zabir wind practices,[1] in a very thorough and detailed way. Immediately his realization and experience burst forth: omniscient wisdom and miraculous powers arose and developed effortlessly. By achieving complete realization of his wind energies and his mind, his miraculous powers enabled him to travel to many holy mountains very easily and without any delay, according to instructions and advice [given to him by Guru Rinpoche and Yeshe Tsogyal]. From the Dakini Assembly Hall of Zhoto Tidro, he received the *Heart Practice of the Lama That Accomplishes All the Sugatas and Fulfills All Wishes*. This was the first terma he revealed.

In a dream, Tsasum Lingpa went to the Pure Land of Lotus Light and had many amazing and inconceivable experiences and visions. From then on, at the holy mountain cave of Chenrezig called Tsari Zilchen Phug, Mön Sha'ug Taggo, Kongne, and other places, he revealed many terma teachings. Because he knew that his root teacher, Könchog Thinley Zangpo, was thinking to benefit all other beings by entering mahaparinirvana, Tsasum Lingpa traveled to see him; but due to obstacles on the path, it took him longer than expected, and when he arrived, his lama had already passed away—it was the day of the cremation. This happened during the same period of time when the Zungar armies invaded central Tibet (around 1718).

Tsasum Lingpa went back to Kham and opened the secret mountain door of Jowo Zegyal, the second Tsari. This was the first of many other secret doors in sacred mountains that he opened. Due to his auspicious connections with the king of Ngachen and other dharma patrons and disciples, his dharma activities were able to spread to some degree in that area of Tibet. In particular, he had very positive connections with the dharma patrons of Kanam Depa in the hidden valley of the Puwo area of Kham. There he founded a small monastery named Dudul Ngagpai Ling, in the valley of Trimzig Ngamchen at Puwo Yegong. On the eastern side of this mountain range, called the Gawalung Valley, he identified the holy site of Hayagriva; in the south, Jala Singdam, the holy site of Yamantaka; in the west, the mountain of Bongri, the holy site of the Dakini; and in the north, Ma Kunglung, the holy site of the Eight Herukas. From Ngamchen Rong, he revealed a large cycle of terma teachings of the Eight Herukas. He also revealed many other terma teachings in this area. He was able to transcribe and spread most of these teachings through empowerment, transmission, and pith instructions.

Tsasum Lingpa recounted his life up to this point in his own autobiography, which is known as the *Clear Garland Crystals of Fire*. Written in verse and comprising more than three hundred loose pages in *pecha* form, it describes his visions, predictions, and songs, although it does not actually include many details about his daily life. It appears that no one contributed any additional information about his life beyond the time when his autobiography ends [when he was about thirty years old].

When he went to the Puwo region, he enthroned Daglha Gampo Zhabdrung as his lineage holder. This was apparently around the time of Zangpo Dorje Tulku.

Tsasum Lingpa has many names: Pema Terdag Lingpa, Karma Ledril Lingpa, Rigdzin Tsasum Lingpa, Garwang Ngachok Dorje, Ngagchang Hungnag Dragtsal, Rigdzin Dudul Dorje, and Terchen Padma Mindrol.

When he went to Samye Chimphu in the village of Chidmo Drong, he practiced with a "qualified lady" as his consort. She gave birth to his son, Rigdzin Thugchog Dorje.[2]

He made a list of his terma teachings while he was in the Puwo area, which include: "Four different long-life practices, the Dark Red Amulet of Yangdag and Phurba, three different practices on wrathful deities, practices on 'the Great Compassionate One,' Lion-Faced Dakini practices, two different practices on Shing Chong, practices on the five emanations of Mahakala, practices on 'the Hundred Thousand Essences of the Mighty One,'

*The protector Jowo Zegyal over the mountain that bears his name in Tibet.
Below is Gochen, the home monastery of the Venerable Khenpos.*

and many others. Altogether, the yellow-scroll termas that I revealed and transcribed up to the Fire Dog year[3] total a little over fourteen volumes." This was said by Tsasum Lingpa himself. This is just a rough list; there are more [terma teachings] than those listed above.

Up to the present day, all of Tsasum Lingpa's terma teachings that include lineage transmission and empowerment are as follows:

1. The *Heart Practice of the Lama Who Embodies All Sugatas,* which includes the *General Practice That Fulfills All Wishes.* Additionally, there are more teachings on the creation- and completion-stage practices, which comprise two volumes. These teachings were revealed from Dragmar Keutsang Cave in Samye Chimphu.

2. The very profound *Guru Dragpoi Yang Zab Padma Tagthung*—the wrathful practice of Guru Rinpoche connected with the *tantra,* pith instructions, and very profound instructions on the four empowerments. These very extraordinary teachings include many details about the four actions and comprise two volumes.

3. The Eight Great Heruka teachings known as *Kagyad Chenmo Sangwa Zilnon,* which include about fourteen different tantra teachings, together with more pith instructions and actions. These very detailed teachings comprise seven volumes. He revealed this terma from the Lotus Hidden Grove in the Ngamchen Rong Forest of Puwo Trimzig.

4. The very profound Dark Red Amulet teachings of Vajrakilaya, which he revealed from Mön Sha'ug Taggo, comprise one volume.

5. He revealed the *Long-Life Practice That Suppresses and Overpowers Yama* from Zhilchen Sangphug of Tsari; the *Long-Life Practice of Vajra Armor* from the rocky mountain of Lho Wazhab, which looks like a long-life vase; and the *Long-Life Practice of Padma Sangting* from the neck of Mount Rinchen Pung Jowo Zegyal in the eastern part of Doshul. The long-life practice known as the *Firm Iron Knot That Prevents Death,* which includes detailed instructions, was revealed in

the Dakini Heart Cave, located at the border of the upper and lower Doshul regions. Altogether, these four practices on Buddha Amitayus comprise about one volume.

6. The practice on Avalokiteshvara, the Great Compassionate One, known as the *Practice That Overpowers Samsara and Nirvana* was revealed in the Lotus Crystal Cave in the hidden valley of Dragge and comprises one volume.

7. He revealed Hayagriva teachings and practices known as *The Essence of the Sun That Enjoys the Supreme Horse* from a boulder that looks like a horse's head at Puwo Darna. Together with this, he revealed the *Condensed Power of the Wrathful Deity Hayagriva*. The practice of Vajrasattva known as *Waves of Light of Wisdom of Dorje Sempa* was revealed from Sirling Norbu Bangdzog in the Riwoche region. He also revealed the *Vajrapani Practices That Dominate All the Mighty Ones* from Lho Chigyud Mugpo Lhatse, also in Riwoche. He revealed the *Sadhana Practice That Prevents Hailstorms*, as well as the dharmapala practices of Brungje Nojin and Goddess Dudsol, all from Sirling Norbu Bangdzog in Riwoche. From the ear of the statue of Buddha Maitreya at Dunchu Monastery, he revealed the wrathful practice of Guru Rinpoche known as *Wangdrag Padma Yangsang*, as well as teachings on Dorje Drolö, which have three different sections. The teachings from Hayagriva to Dorje Drolö [listed here as no. 7] comprise one volume.

8. The wrathful Manjushri practice called *Blazing Poisonous Lava Mountain and the Frightening Vajra* was revealed from the Ngamchen Rong Valley and comprises one volume.

9. *The Secret Dakini Practice That Fulfills All Wishes* together with many action practices were revealed from the Secret Dakini Cave of Drigung Zhotod Tidro Dragkar and comprise one volume.

10. He revealed the *Lion-Faced Dakini Practice That Subdues All Devils*,

which comprises about one volume, from the Dark Red Glacial Lake of Jowo Zegyal Mountain.

11. The *Sing Chug Gonpo* practices, which comprise about half a volume, were revealed from glorious Tsari Mountain.

12. *The Wealth Deity Practice of Guru Pema Gyalpo*, which is very detailed and elaborate, was revealed from the mountain of Lagong Genyen in the Chamdo region.

13. *The Black Mountain of the Devil Caste*, otherwise known as *The Wish-Fulfilling Jewel Treasure Mountain*, is a wrathful practice on Guru Rinpoche that will prevent and reverse the invasion of the *thamag duruka*, the armies of "foreign smokers." These last two teachings [nos. 12 and 13] comprise one volume.

Each of these terma teachings is a comfortable, convenient length of about 250 pages; altogether, they total about eighteen medium-sized volumes that resonate with the living lineages of empowerment and transmission. There are many more termas that could not be transcribed from the yellow scrolls. In addition, it appears that some of the termas, even though they were transcribed, do not currently have any empowerment and transmission lineages.

This brief biography of the great tertön Tsasum Lingpa was written by Jamyang Khyentse Pema Ösel Dongnag Lingpa in the middle of the nineteenth century. It was translated by Khenpo Tsewang Dongyal and Pema Dragpa in the Shantarakshita Library of the Sambhogakaya Temple at Padma Samye Ling, in the seventh month of the Fire Dog year, August 2006. May all be auspicious!

Vajrakilaya according to the Tsasum Lingpa lineage teachings

CHAPTER I

The Empowerment of Vajrakilaya

In order to receive the empowerment[4] of Vajrakilaya, a practitioner first needs to have the right motivation, which is based upon *bodhichitta*. *Bodhichitta* is a Sanskrit word meaning "enlightenment mind" or "enlightenment thought" that encompasses the vast motivation of great compassion, love, and wisdom. Through bodhichitta, one's mind becomes open toward every single sentient being.

This attitude is applied by thinking that you are receiving the empowerment for the sake of all sentient beings: "I am determined to follow the path to enlightenment by means of the practice of Vajrakilaya. My practice is dedicated to the benefit of all beings so that they may have whatever they need, their suffering will be removed, and their enlightenment will be invoked." This is the motivation that needs to be developed.

In addition to bodhichitta, clear interest and devotion toward Vajrakilaya and his entire *mandala* are necessary. The student's readiness is also an important factor when receiving this empowerment.

Empowerment in this context has two meanings: removing or expelling and receiving or pouring. You are removing the four levels of obscurations: outer, inner, secret, and very subtle; this is done by receiving the four stages of the blessings of the empowerment. The four *vajra* states—vajra body, vajra speech, vajra mind, and vajra totality—can be actualized through the Vajrakilaya empowerment.

This empowerment combines two deities, Vajrakilaya and Yangdag (or Samyag) Heruka, whose practices were combined by Guru Padmasambhava.

The empowerment of Vajrakilaya and Yangdag Heruka is one of the most profound and secret empowerments because it combines the three inner tantras.

Buddha Shakyamuni gave many levels of teachings so that all sentient beings would be able to reach enlightenment. Among his teachings are the three inner tantras: Mahayoga, Anuyoga, and Atiyoga. Mahayoga focuses on establishing the entire universe as the mandala of the deities. Anuyoga focuses on actualizing the vajra body; one's physical condition is seen as the vajra city of the wrathful and peaceful deities. Atiyoga focuses on revealing one's own primordial-awareness wisdom. This Vajrakilaya practice combines all three inner tantras in a single practice.

This particular teaching was given by Buddha Shakyamuni—in the form of the wrathful buddha Vajrakilaya himself—in the pure land known as the "Secret Charnel Ground of Blazing Fire" or "The Blazing Mandala."[5] Buddha Shakyamuni as Vajrakilaya gave this teaching to many *vidyadharas* (supreme awareness holders), including the wrathful *dakas* and *dakinis* (male and female wisdom beings). This teaching was then given to great masters such as Garab Dorje, Manjushrimitra (Jampal Shenyen), Shri Singha, Vimalamitra, and the second buddha, Guru Padmasambhava.

When Vimalamitra and Guru Padmasambhava came to Tibet, they gave this transmission to many students. One of the foremost students to receive this teaching was the wisdom dakini Yeshe Tsogyal, who attained enlightenment within her lifetime. Guru Padmasambhava also transmitted it to King Trisong Deutsen and his queens and ministers, so that it spread in all directions. Many lineages of Vajrakilaya practice developed, including those of Yeshe Tsogyal, King Trisong Deutsen, and other masters such as Nanam. The phurba teachings became the most powerful and famous teachings in Tibetan Buddhist history.

Within the Nyingma lineage, there are three or six lineages of transmission, based on different methods of transferring the teachings to students. The first lineage is the *dharmakaya* method of the mind-to-mind transmission of the victorious ones, which is the transference of the teachings from one realized mind to another. The second is the *sambhogakaya* method of the symbolic transmission lineage of the vidyadharas, and the third is the *nirmanakaya* method of the oral transmission lineage of individuals. When the Nyingma lineage teachings arrived in Tibet, they were transferred in three additional ways: through the lineage handed down by the dakinis, through the aspiration and initiation lineage, and through the inherited or predicted lineage. This Vajrakilaya teaching contains all six of these lineage transmissions.

Guru Padmasambhava and the wisdom dakini Yeshe Tsogyal predicted that around the seventeenth century a famous tertön (treasure revealer) known as Tsasum Lingpa would reveal these hidden Vajrakilaya teachings. After he discovered this terma, Tsasum Lingpa gave the transmission of these teachings to his students. From that time until the present day, this teaching has been transmitted in an unbroken lineage.

Both the Kama and Terma lineages contain many Vajrakilaya teachings. The combination of Yangdag Heruka and Vajrakilaya is quite rare within the Terma tradition. It is one of the most precious teachings of Guru Padmasambhava and one of the most extraordinary teachings of the Nyingma lineage.

PROTECTION-BOUNDARY MEDITATION

Before beginning the actual practice of Vajrakilaya, certain things are necessary. First, we must have the right motivation, which is based upon loving-kindness, compassion, and bodhichitta, along with devotion and pure perception. With that correct motivation, we take refuge and develop the thought of enlightenment, and then meditate on the *sung khor*, the protection wheel or boundary.

From the point of view of reality, everything is totally enlightened. Whatever we see and perceive is the display of awareness wisdom because everything is already in a completely awakened state. The four actions are completely accomplished; they are beyond conceptions, so there is no one to protect and nothing that needs to be protected. However, in our world of mundane conceptions we have dualistic thoughts of subject and object, of "me" and "you." As long as we have these concepts, it is important to meditate on the protection boundary.

This meditation is based upon the pure understanding of phenomena known as pure perception, which is the view of the Vajrayana (also known as the view of the mandala and the view of the entirely pure state). Meditation on the protection wheel or boundary can be summarized according to the two truths: relative truth and absolute truth.

According to relative truth, bodhichitta meditation focuses on loving-kindness, compassion, and bodhichitta. First there is loving-kindness and then compassion, and the union of these two is bodhichitta. As you expand this meditation on love, compassion, and bodhichitta, it includes every sentient being. In this way, all sentient beings become equal with yourself, and you do not see any real difference between you and them. When you understand that they are just as important as you are, then you are willing to share your joy and peace with them. You are able to exchange your own happiness for their suffering, bad situations, and trouble. This is *tonglen*, the exchanging practice.

By doing this practice, eventually you will feel that all beings are not only equal to you, but actually more precious to you than yourself. Practicing on bodhichitta matures one's capacity to equalize and exchange, and then to feel that others are more important than oneself. This is why the protection-boundary meditation is very special and powerful.

Loving-kindness, compassion, and bodhichitta comprise the essential teaching of Buddha Shakyamuni within the Mahayana and the six levels of tantra. For that reason, Guru Padmasambhava taught that these three are the realized mind of the Buddha. When you are meditating on pure love, pure compassion, and bodhichitta, you are actualizing Buddha's enlightened mind.

The practice of the protection-boundary meditation according to absolute truth is not very different from that according to relative truth. In Buddhist philosophy, the ultimate nature is also named bodhichitta. In the Sutra Mahayana, there are two aspects of bodhichitta: relative and absolute. These two aspects of bodhichitta are completely related. By practicing the relative bodhichitta meditation, you will be close to absolute truth. You cannot find absolute bodhichitta without relative bodhichitta, even if you look for one hundred eons.

With regard to the meditation of *Dzogchen*, "the great perfection" (Dzogpa Chenpo), the view is bodhichitta. For example, in the famous Atiyoga tantra *The Bodhichitta That Is the King of All Creation*[6] "bodhichitta" is also a synonym for the Dzogchen view. Another example of this can be found in the teachings of Garab Dorje, the first master of the Dzogchen lineage. After Garab Dorje transformed into the wisdom rainbow body, he transmitted his legacy teaching to his foremost student, Manjushrimitra. When Manjushrimitra subsequently transcribed this teaching, he entitled it "The Meditation on Bodhichitta," although it is actually a teaching about Dzogchen. He described it as a teaching about how to meditate on bodhichitta.

Bodhichitta is very important in all its aspects—these practices are essential for everyone who wishes to attain enlightenment. Relative bodhichitta and absolute bodhichitta are completely related to each other. One of them cannot be discarded while the other one is accepted because both are integral for attaining enlightenment.

As long as every aspect of your dharma practice is mingled with bodhichitta, then your practice is going in the right direction. All the teachings of Buddha Shakyamuni are based upon bodhichitta; in fact, the eighty-four thousand different teachings are all branches of this one root. If you have bodhichitta, then undoubtedly you will reach enlightenment. If you do not have bodhichitta, no matter what sophisticated techniques you may use, your realization will be delayed, and the techniques will simply hide your enlightened nature.

To meditate on the protection boundary from the absolute point of view, first it is necessary to ask, "Who is it that needs to be protected?" Perhaps you feel, "I am the one who needs protection." But who is this "I"? This is what needs to be examined.

The notion of the "I" is simply our imagination. We label and name an "I" because we have the combination and continuation of the five aggregates. Of course, when we do not examine this, it looks as though a self exists. If we look carefully (not just outwardly), and inwardly focus and search through every aspect of the five aggregates, we are not going to find any "I." Looking from the gross level to the subtle level, and from the subtle level to the finest atoms, there is no such thing as an "I" to be found.

Not only the personal self, but also everything we cling to, both outwardly and inwardly, is based upon emptiness. From beginningless time, the entire universe and all existing phenomena have been based upon great emptiness. We came from emptiness, we are within emptiness, and we will dissolve back into emptiness. Our entire passage, our situation, and our existence are within this great nature.

While the entire universe is arising, it is also dissolving. Arising, existing, and dissolving are like magical displays. Nothing exists solidly or permanently; everything is moving and changing within great emptiness, like a movie or a magic show that we can watch. Great emptiness is also known as great openness, in which everything has room to act and is inseparable from the totality of emptiness.

To see this situation clearly, at first it is necessary to contemplate upon this great emptiness. After recognizing the reality of great emptiness, we need to maintain that recognition by meditating on the absolute truth. What meditation actually means according to the Buddhist point of view is simply maintaining the natural state. Other than the natural state, there is nothing to meditate upon. Continuously maintaining the true nature is the greatest protection meditation. There is no higher protection boundary than this.

Generally, since we have such strong habitual patterns of clinging to phenomena and to an "I," it is necessary to do the protection-boundary meditation on the relative level as well. This meditation is based on love, compassion, and bodhichitta, while the meditation on the absolute level is based on the natural state.

To practice this meditation step-by-step, begin with the relative-truth protection boundary as follows. Hold good posture and visualize white light radiating from your heart center. This white light is the combination of pure love, pure compassion, and bodhichitta. Visualize it shining in all directions and touching all sentient beings. It purifies their obscurations and actualizes their thoughts of loving-kindness and compassion for each other. Then, visualize the white light coming back to you. At the very moment it returns, you are transformed into Avalokiteshvara, who is the embodiment of the compassion of all the buddhas of the ten directions and the three times. Then chant the mantra of Avalokiteshvara twenty-one times.

Next, meditate on absolute bodhichitta—the great emptiness, the true nature—by using a Vajrayana technique. Consider yourself as you ordinarily are and hold good posture. From your heart center, arising from the primordial nature, golden light radiates in every direction and touches all the beings of the six realms. This golden light removes all their obscurations and ignorance, just as the sun dispels darkness. Maintain that clarity, that great view, and that openness for about five minutes.

Having purified all obscurations and ignorance, the golden light returns to you and instantly you are transformed into Manjushri, who is the embodiment of the wisdom of all the buddhas of the ten directions and the three times. With that thought, recite the mantra of Manjushri twenty-one times.

Next, the combination of relative bodhichitta and absolute bodhichitta appears in the form of blue light that radiates from your heart center in all directions to all sentient beings of the six realms. It purifies and completely dispels their obstacles, negativities, and emotional problems. Meditate in this way for about five minutes.

The light returns as before, and instantly you are transformed into Vajrapani, the embodiment of the power of all the buddhas of the ten directions and the three times. Vajrapani does not differ from Vajrakilaya; in fact, Vajrakilaya is sometimes called the more wrathful aspect of Vajrapani. Meditating thusly, recite the mantra of Vajrapani twenty-one times.

If you are unfamiliar with Avalokiteshvara, Manjushri, or Vajrapani, simply visualize that the light returns after completing the buddhas' activities.

This is the general way of meditating on the protection wheel or boundary. When practicing the Vajrakilaya sadhana, it is not necessary to include this meditation every time, but generally it is a very good practice to do.

PURE PERCEPTION

The Vajrayana teachings are very profound, very secret, and very vast—they are like the ocean, like the earth, and like the sky. In the Vajrayana, the pith instructions are especially important because the practitioner needs to know how to collect and put together the essential teachings to be practiced. Sadhana practice is the essence of the Vajrayana, as it is the result or fruit of the tantric teachings.

Whenever you receive a Vajrayana teaching or do Vajrayana practice, it is very important to have the attitude of pure perception. Pure perception can be understood through the five perfections.

The first perfection is the perfect place. Wherever we are is the pure land, a realm beyond concepts called "Ogmin" in Tibetan, or "Akanishta" in Sanskrit. This realm is the same as the pure land of Vajrakilaya, the abovementioned "Secret Charnel Ground of Blazing Fire."

The second perfection involves seeing the perfect teacher as none other than Vajrakilaya. Your own primordial nature—the nature of your awareness—is none other than Vajrakilaya or Vajrakumara (Dorje Phurba and Dorje Zhönu,[7] respectively). Your teacher is none other than Vajrakilaya, you are none other than Vajrakilaya, and everyone is an emanation of Vajrakilaya. All sentient beings are in the awakened state. This perfection is the perfect understanding of the perfect teacher.

The third perfection is the perfect teaching. The Buddha Vajrakilaya turned the wheel of the Kilaya teachings one hundred thousand times. One of the most famous Kilaya teachings, the *Vidyottama Tantra*,[8] reveals the primordial nature and is taught unceasingly to sentient beings throughout the three times. All sounds, all echoes, and all voices are none other than the sound of supreme awareness.

The fourth perfection is the perfect retinue, which is the manifestation or wisdom display of Vajrakilaya. The members of this retinue are not ordinary disciples; they are all great bodhisattvas, both male and female. Or, in Vajrayana terms, they are the male and female vidyadharas—the holders of supreme awareness. Having pure perception, you will see everyone as vidyadharas.

The fifth perfection is the perfect time. The other four perfections are within the perfect time, which is beyond the three times. The perfect time, known as the fourth time or primordial time, is beyond all conceptions and fabrications, and beyond arising and ceasing. The perfect time is always there, abiding without changing.

This is a brief explanation of the five perfections. When you receive or practice the inner tantra teachings, it is necessary to have this pure understanding. Everything in this world, whether external or internal, is based on these perfections. In order to reveal this understanding, we need to have vajra courage. Rather than hovering on the surface of confusion and ignorance, we need to invoke these hidden qualities. We can transform every aspect of ignorance into these five perfections, which are the original reality. Through the practice of Vajrakilaya, we are going to reveal the actual nature of existence.

Guru Padmasambhava

CHAPTER 2

History of the Vajrakilaya Transmission

The Vajrakilaya transmission is a very profound, vast, and high tantric teaching that can be divided into three, six, or nine lineages. As the six or nine lineages are included within the main three lineages, the Vajrakilaya transmission can be discussed in terms of these three lineages.

The first lineage is the mind-to-mind transmission lineage of the victorious ones, the second is the symbolic transmission lineage of the vidyadharas, and the third is the oral transmission lineage of individuals.

MIND-TO-MIND TRANSMISSION LINEAGE

The mind-to-mind transmission lineage of the victorious ones is beyond concepts, beyond all our ideas and discriminations. At the present time, all our thoughts and actions are within the realm of concepts. The Dzogchen teachings state that any activities we perform will increase our habitual patterns and concepts. No matter what we analyze, contemplate, or try to do, whether it is profound, high, or low, it will always add to our conceptual complexity.

The mind-to-mind transmission lineage is the mind of the victorious ones, which is beyond all complexities and concepts. It is the totally enlightened state. Being beyond duality, it is the dharmakaya—the realized mind of the buddhas. In the state of great equality, there is no such thing as a male buddha or a female buddha. Those discriminations exist only within the realm of concepts.

The nondual state is known by different names, such as the dharma-kaya or the svabhavakaya. These different descriptions exist only on the conceptual level. Ultimately, this state cannot be divided.

The great vastness that is the dharmakaya is not totally blank or void. From the dharmakaya, all kinds of manifestations occur without any effort or thought. They are not separate from or different than the dharmakaya; they are manifestations of the potential of the primordial nature. According to the Dzogchen teachings, from the nonexisting nature—from the basic nature that is nothing whatsoever—all kinds of things arise naturally. Since things do not need to be created forcefully by someone, they are spontaneous. The nature of this spontaneity is known as *rigpa*, which is the nature of primordial wisdom. From that wisdom energy the five wisdoms naturally arise, and they are reflected as the five dhyani buddhas and all the vidyadharas.

When we do not have a profound understanding of reality, in the ordinary world the five wisdoms appear as the five aggregates, the five elements, the five colors, and the five poisons. Those conceptions arise because they suit our deluded thinking. In reality they are none other than the five wisdoms or the five dhyani buddhas.

Whether they appear as the five wisdoms and the five buddhas, or as the five poisons and the five aggregates, the five wisdoms are based upon the same primordial nature—the great dharmakaya. In whatever form, place, or time they arise, there is not one atom that goes beyond the primordial state. This is the essence of the profound true nature. However, because we are deluded by dualistic perceptions, we make distinctions between subject and object, and when we hold on to those notions, we create many different things around us.

To protect beings from this kind of delusion, the buddhas appear in many different forms. For example, among the various emanations are the buddha families of the five directions. The eastern buddha is Vajrasattva, the southern buddha is Ratnasambhava, the western buddha is Amitabha, the northern buddha is Amoghasiddhi, and the central buddha is Vairochana. On the absolute level, there is just one emanation of primordial wisdom; ultimately, there are no different levels. But in order to help remove our dualistic concepts or to dispel our ignorance, they appear as different buddhas. These buddha families are not separate families who exist in the various directions, such as the vajra family, the rich family who lives in the east, and the padma family, the aristocratic family in the west; that is not the point. They appear this way in order to lead sentient beings to nondual wisdom.

These symbols of wisdom are used to illustrate profound meaning. For example, the buddhas appear as peaceful, wrathful, or semiwrathful, and as male or female. In terms of symbolism, the eight great male bodhisattvas represent the transmutation of the eight consciousnesses. The eight great female bodhisattvas represent the transformation of the objects of the eight consciousnesses. The four gatekeepers are the transmutation of the four extreme views about existence and nonexistence. They all have symbolic meanings.

This particular teaching is about the Buddha Vajrakilaya. In some tantras Vajrakilaya is described as the wrathful transformation of Vajradhara and in other tantras as the wrathful transformation of Vajrasattva. However, there is no contradiction between Vajradhara and Vajrasattva, as they represent the same nature.

Buddha Vajradhara is said to be the lord of the six buddha families. The five families are as mentioned above, and the sixth family is the source of the other five families. The sixth family is the enlightened mind beyond dualistic concepts. Vajradhara is the lord of the five buddha families as well as their source. All six families are none other than primordial wisdom. Vajradhara is also none other than Buddha Samantabhadra, who is the embodiment of primordial wisdom—clarity and emptiness.

Samantabhadra is sometimes referred to as the dharmakaya buddha, and Vajradhara as the sambhogakaya buddha. Yet Vajradhara is also referred to as a dharmakaya buddha. This is not a contradiction; it simply illustrates the divisions within the mind-to-mind transmission lineage. Within the primordial nature, the primordial-wisdom aspect is referred to as Samantabhadra and the clarity aspect is referred to as Vajradhara; they are two aspects of one single nature. In this way, Samantabhadra can be considered the dharmakaya aspect and Vajradhara the sambhogakaya aspect.

There are many ways of looking at the mind-to-mind transmission lineage. In the higher Nyingma tantras distinctions are made, for example, by dividing the dharmakaya into three levels: the dharmakaya of the dharmakaya, the dharmakaya of the sambhogakaya, and the dharmakaya of the nirmanakaya. Hence, the dharmakaya of the dharmakaya is Samantabhadra, the dharmakaya of the sambhogakaya is Vajradhara, and the dharmakaya of the nirmanakaya is Vajrasattva. All three are in the dharmakaya.

When Vajradhara and Vajrasattva are transformed into their wrathful aspects, they are Vajrakilaya. The main purpose of the emanation of Vajrakilaya is to help sentient beings remove their dualistic conceptions. Therefore, his emanation appears in many different ways. For instance, his body, his arms, his hand implements, his colors, and so forth can all be different. The *Vidyottama Tantra* states that there are many types of emanations of Vajrakilaya.

According to another Vajrakilaya tantra, the *Secret Tantra of Vajrakilaya*,[9] Vajrakilaya has one thousand heads, one thousand arms, and one million eyes. The *Nirvana Tantra of Vajrakilaya*[10] states that Vajrakilaya has nine heads, eighteen arms, and eight legs. In the *Root Tantra of the Wrathful Vajra*[11] Vajrakilaya has three heads, six arms, and four legs. In the *Twelve Kilayas Tantra*[12] Vajrakilaya has one face, two arms, and two legs. In all these tantras, Vajrakilaya also has wings. Thus, we can see that there are different emanations of Vajrakilaya in the different tantras. No matter what form he takes, there is always a similarity with the human form. He has a head, arms, legs, and so forth. But when Vajrakilaya appears to non-human beings, he looks completely different and appears in a marvelous and unimaginable way.

SYMBOLIC TRANSMISSION LINEAGE

The source of the emanations of Vajrakilaya is the dharmakaya, the realm of the mind-to-mind transmission lineage. The dharmakaya is reflected as Vajrakilaya in the sambhogakaya, the realm of the symbolic transmission lineage of the vidyadharas. Arising from Samantabhadra or the dharmakaya, Vajrasattva or the sambhogakaya is wrathfully transformed into Vajrakilaya. The dharmakaya and sambhogakaya, the mind-to-mind transmission lineage and the symbolic transmission lineage, are beyond our conceptions. We may ask, "Where is Vajrakilaya, or where is Vajradhara?" The answer would be that they are in the Ogmin pure land or Akanishta, which means "not under dualistic conceptions." According to the Dzogchen teachings, the Ogmin palace is beyond all dualistic categories and characteristics.

If you ask for the permanent address of Vajradhara or Samantabhadra, or you want to know the telephone number of Vajrakilaya, we always say they are in Akanishta, the palace of the dharmadhatu. Sometimes, in order to make it suit our concepts, we say they reside in a palace. When we think of a palace where tourists go, such as Queen Elizabeth's palace, we think of something very fancy and nice, so we can apply that to the dharmadhatu and call it the Ogmin palace.

Vajrakilaya is within the sambhogakaya, which is beyond concepts. According to the three transmission lineages in the Nyingma School, Samantabhadra, Vajradhara, Vajrasattva, and Vajrakilaya belong to the mind-to-mind transmission lineage as well as the symbolic transmission lineage.

ORAL TRANSMISSION LINEAGE

We live in a world of dualistic concepts, subjects, and objects where we are clinging and grasping. How did we find out about the state beyond concepts? Through the lineage called the individual oral transmission lineage.

Vajrakilaya unceasingly teaches the Vajrakilaya tantras in the "Secret Charnel Ground of Blazing Fire." There are two major lineages describing how this teaching came to this world in the nonhuman and human realms.

These teachings were transmitted in the nonhuman realms by the three great buddhas or bodhisattvas: Manjushri, Avalokiteshvara, and Vajrapani. Manjushri gave the transmission in the god realms, and hundreds of thousands of gods reached the vidyadhara level through the practice of Vajrakilaya. Avalokiteshvara gave these teachings in the naga realms, and hundreds of thousands of *nagas* reached the vidyadhara level through this practice. Vajrapani gave these teachings to the *rakshas* or cannibal demons, and *yakshas* or harmful demons, and hundreds of thousands of them also attained the vidyadhara level through Vajrakilaya practice.

With regard to how these teachings appeared in the human realm, according to one history, about fifty years after the Buddha Shakyamuni's mahaparinirvana, in the western part of India known as Udiyana there was a remarkable emanation named Hasya Vajra or Garab Dorje who received teachings directly from Vajrasattva. These included the Vajrakilaya teachings, and Garab Dorje collected and preserved these teachings by transcribing and summarizing them, and writing commentaries on them.

According to another history, Buddha Shakyamuni himself taught the Vajrakilaya tantras. Within the mind-to-mind transmission lineage or the dharmakaya, Buddha Shakyamuni and Vajrakilaya are the same basic nature, without any distinctions or differences in realization. Buddha Shakyamuni as Vajrakilaya gave one hundred thousand different Kilaya teachings, which are condensed in the *Vidyottama Tantra*. There are many different teachings on Vajrakilaya.

After the Buddha turned the wheel of the Vajrakilaya teachings, he entrusted them to two *dharmapalas* (dharma protectors), Vajrapani and wisdom dakini Lekyi Wangmo. There are various histories of how Vajrapani and Lekyi Wangmo passed on the teachings. According to our literal way of thinking, twenty-eight years after Buddha Shakyamuni passed into parinirvana, five great masters met on the peak of a "meteorite" mountain[13] and prayed longingly to all the buddhas of the ten directions. Their prayers contained twenty-three different statements. When they finished their prayers, Vajrapani appeared in the sky in front of them and conferred all of the Vajrayana teachings. One of the five masters, Lodrö Tabden, wrote them down using gold ink on paper made of lapis lazuli. He then hid those writings in the sky by means of his seven powers of realization, and about one hundred years later the wisdom dakini Lekyi Wangmo discovered these teachings and transmitted them to the Eight Great Vidyadharas.

Another history recounts that about fifty years after Buddha Shakyamuni's parinirvana, Vajrapani and Lekyi Wangmo hid the Vajrakilaya teachings in the Deche Tsegpa stupa.[14] After the teachings were hidden, during the daytime the stupa would emit smoke, and at night it would glow with flames.

When the time came for those teachings to be revealed, Guru Padmasambhava and the Eight Great Vidyadharas[15] gathered spontaneously at the Deche Tsegpa stupa. There was no need to call each other to schedule the meeting; they simply arrived at the same time and the same place.

When they arrived, Lekyi Wangmo appeared to them. She already knew their intention, but she asked them, "Why have you come here? What do you need? What can I do for you?" They said, "We have come to reveal the special teachings. Please give them to us." She handed a small casket to each of the eight vidyadharas, and inside each casket was one of the Eight Great Heruka teachings. Along with the tantras, she gave the full transmission, initiation, and instructions to each of them.

The great master Manjushrimitra received the iron casket that held the special transmission of Yamantaka, including the *Secret Manjushri Tantra*.[16] These are the buddha family teachings on the body of all the buddhas. The great master Nagarjuna received the copper casket containing the transmission of the padma family speech teachings, including the *Supreme Hayagriva Root Tantra*.[17] The great vidyadhara Hungkara received the crystal casket containing the transmission of Yangdag Heruka, including the *Powerful Heruka Tantra*.[18] These are the vajra family teachings on the mind of all the buddhas.

The great masters Guru Padmasambhava and Prabhahasti were given the bone casket, or (some say) the turquoise casket, and inside it were the Vajrakilaya tantras, including the *Vidyottama Tantra*, the karma family teachings on the activity of all the buddhas.

The great master Vimalamitra received the gold casket containing the *Amrita Tantras*, the tantras on the qualities of all the buddhas. The great master Dhanasamskrita received the red-gold casket containing the *mamo* or dakini tantras, including the *Gyülung Bumtig Tantra*,[19] the "essence of one hundred thousand tantras with oral instructions." The great master

Rombuguhya Devachandra received the garnet casket containing the *Tantra of All the Mighty Ones*,[20] the tantra that explains how to control the hearts of powerful worldly beings. The great vidyadhara Shantigarbha received the casket made of *dzi*, a stone marked with stripes or "eyes" that is considered the most precious stone in Tibet. Inside that casket was the *Möpa Drag Ngag Tantra*,[21] the "tantra of targeted, powerful mantra" which includes the *White Crystal Mala of Wrathful Mantras* teaching.

The great master Padmasambhava received the casket made of eight precious metals containing a condensed, complete transmission of all the Eight Herukas, the *Embodiment of All the Sugatas*.[22] When the dakini Lekyi Wangmo revealed this combined teaching of the Eight Herukas to Guru Padmasambhava, there was even more lightning, fire, and smoke around the stupa. Then, Guru Padmasambhava himself gave this combined teaching to the Eight Great Vidyadharas.

Guru Padmasambhava received the Eight Heruka sadhanas from the eight vidyadharas as well as from Lekyi Wangmo. In particular, he received the Vajrakilaya transmission from both Prabhahasti and Lekyi Wangmo. Guru Padmasambhava is known as the master of all the Eight Herukas and particularly as the master of Vajrakilaya.

The lineages of the Eight Herukas, including Vajrakilaya, originated in India.[23] Along with these Eight Heruka sadhanas and tantras, there is a ninth tantra called the *Guru Vidyadhara Tantra*,[24] which also combines the Eight Herukas. Guru Padmasambhava brought this tantra along with the other heruka tantras to Tibet.

This is how the Vajrakilaya teachings began in this world. There are many other stories of how this lineage was transmitted, but all of them have come down to us through Guru Padmasambhava as the master of the Eight Herukas.

After Guru Padmasambhava received the Vajrakilaya teachings, he practiced in the cave at Yangleshöd[25] before he came to Tibet. Although he was already enlightened, he did this to demonstrate the need for practice. Guru Padmasambhava's practice on Vajrakilaya was one of his supreme beneficial activities.

At Yangleshöd, he was doing the practice of Yangdag Heruka, the Samyag Sambuddha, which is known as the mind family of the buddhas. The Yangdag Heruka practice begins with the nine-lamp Yangdag practice.[26] During that time many obstacles were arising in Nepal. There was a severe drought, and as a result, no crops had grown. There was a great amount of lightning, and many other external obstacles manifested.

Guru Padmasambhava felt that he needed more Vajrakilaya instructions at this time, so he sent a Nepalese couple to the monastery at Nalanda where Prabhahasti was still living. This couple, Jila Jisa and Kunla Kunsa, received the texts from Prabhahasti and brought them back to Guru Padmasambhava at Yangleshöd. To subdue all the obstacles, Guru Padmasambhava invoked the power of the Buddha in the form of Vajrakilaya.

The moment Guru Padmasambhava began to practice Vajrakilaya, all the negativity was completely pacified. By combining the practices of Yangdag Heruka and Vajrakilaya, he subdued the three most powerful local spirits, Lu Jungpo, Nöjin Gömakha, and Barnong Lomatrin, and he caused the rain to fall. When Guru Padmasambhava subdued these spirits through his practice, the power of Vajrakilaya subdued the spirits of the earth, the sky, and the area between the earth and sky. He continued the practice of combining Vajrakilaya and Yangdag Heruka for three years. From the perspective of ordinary history, Guru Padmasambhava proclaimed that he reached the Mahamudra[27] realization of enlightenment by practicing Vajrakilaya at Yangleshöd. Of course, he was already an enlightened being, but he demonstrated this realization to glorify the power and blessings of Vajrakilaya and Yangdag Heruka. At that time Guru Padmasambhava was known as Dorje Tötrengtsal.

Two other great masters, Balpo Shilamanzu and Vimalamitra, subsequently joined him at Yangleshöd to practice Vajrakilaya. According to history, after their practice they revealed various signs of their realization. When a sandalwood forest fire was burning on a nearby mountain, Guru Padmasambhava pointed his phurba at the fire, and it was immediately extinguished, and all the trees returned. Vimalamitra pointed a phurba at the River Ganges and made the waters part, stopping the flow of the river for some time. This was a sign that inwardly Vimalamitra was able to subdue the nagas (water spirits) through his Dorje Phurba practice. Shilamanzu pointed a phurba toward a solid rock mountain called Shilgongdrag,[28] and split the mountain into hundreds of pieces. This showed that inwardly he was able to subdue the demons and spirits of the earth. Guru Padmasambhava, Vimalamitra, and Shilamanzu are known as very powerful masters of Vajrakilaya.

The wisdom dakini Yeshe Tsogyal received the Vajrakilaya teaching from all three of these great masters. She collected their teachings in a book called *The Black Hundred Thousand,*[29] and the way she assembled it is quite wonderful. Instead of simply dividing the text into chapters, she went through the root tantra line by line, explaining what each of the three masters had said about the meaning of each point. In this way, she brought the lineages of Guru Padmasambhava, Vimalamitra, and Shilamanzu together.

When Guru Padmasambhava came to Tibet, he subdued all the negative forces and blessed the entire land. He consecrated the ground and conducted a special groundbreaking ceremony at the place where Samye Monastery was built. According to the inner or secret history, he transformed himself into Vajrakilaya in order to subdue all the negative forces and thus blessed all of Tibet through the power of his meditation on Vajrakilaya.

Guru Padmasambhava also brought the teachings of the Eight Herukas to Tibet. In a cave at Samye Chimphu, he emanated the great mandala of the Eight Herukas, the wrathful practice called *Embodiment of All the Sugatas,* and gave the outer, inner, and secret empowerments on these teachings to his nine heartlike students. During the empowerment, each student threw a golden flower onto the mandala (each direction of the mandala is associated with a particular heruka). The students were given specific heruka teachings corresponding to the directions in which their flowers fell.

The golden flowers of Dharma King Trisong Deutsen and Nyag Jnanakumara fell into the center of the mandala, so they received the teachings on Chemchog Heruka. Ngenlam Gyalwa Chogyang's flower fell in the western direction of the mandala, so he received the Padma Heruka teachings. The flower of Nub Namkhai Nyingpo fell in the eastern direction, and he received the teachings on the mind mandala of Yangdag Heruka. Nub Sangye Yeshe Rinpoche's flower landed in the southern direction, and he received the transmission of the mandala of Yamantaka.

The flower of the princess of Kharchen, Yeshe Tsogyal, fell in the northern direction, so she received the teachings on the mandala of buddha activity, Vajrakilaya. The flower of Drogmi Palgyi Yeshe fell in the southeast direction, and he received the teachings on the mandala of the inciting and dispatching of the mamos.[30] Langchen Palgyi Senge's flower fell in the northwest, and he received teachings on the mandala of offering and praise to worldly deities.[31] The flower of Pagor Vairochana landed in the northeast direction, and he received the teachings on the mandala of the worldly deities of exorcism.[32]

The southwest direction is associated with Guru Padmasambhava himself and the teachings of the *Guru Vidyadhara Tantra*. Through their connection with Guru Padmasambhava, all of his students had a connection with the southwest direction. The nine heartlike students practiced, meditated, and actualized enlightenment within their lifetimes by practicing the sadhanas of the Eight Herukas. Guru Padmasambhava gave the Eight Heruka teachings to his twenty-five main students as well as others. Vajrakilaya was a special teaching of his, and it has been a very special dharma teaching for all Tibetans. Looking at the history of the great masters, we can see that it was through the practice of Vajrakilaya that many of them reached enlightenment.

For example, Guru Padmasambhava gave the Vajrakilaya transmission to King Trisong Deutsen, whose lineage is known as the King lineage. After accomplishing the practice of Vajrakilaya, King Trisong Deutsen pointed a phurba at Hepo Ri Mountain, and when he did so, the mountain caught fire.

Yeshe Tsogyal reached enlightenment through the practice of Vajrakilaya, so she is known as the famous yogini of Vajrakilaya. In particular, she practiced Vajrakilaya for twenty-one days at Mönkha Neuring Senge Dzong (the "Lion's Nest")[33] in eastern Bhutan. She had twenty-one ritual phurbas on her shrine, and at the end of her retreat they started to dance and fly in the sky. At that time she was able to perform the activity of subduing all the negativity and obstacles connected with her family lineage. She also had the ability to bring the dead back to life.

Guru Padmasambhava's student Namkhai Nyingpo practiced Vajrakilaya particularly in Lhodrag, the area in southern Tibet where Marpa the translator was born. After Namkhai Nyingpo attained realization through the practice of Vajrakilaya, he pressed a wooden phurba into solid rock. To this day one can see the print of his phurba on that rock. Nub Sangye Yeshe Rinpoche also left a phurba print at Drag Yangdzong, where its marks are still visible.

Nanam Dorje Dudjom, a student of Guru Padmasambhava who became a great master, pointed a phurba at the Tsangpo River near Lhasa and stopped its flow through the power of Vajrakilaya. Another student, Chim Shakya Prabha, pointed a phurba at some rock boulders, which came together and stacked one above the other. This formation can still be seen today.

Many Vajrakilaya lineages developed from Guru Padmasambhava's teachings in Tibet. The Vajrakilaya lineage of Yeshe Tsogyal is known as the *jomo* lineage, the lineage of the lady. There are many other lineages, such as the King lineage, the Nyag lineage, the Khön lineage, the Rog lineage, the So lineage, the Nub lineage, and so on. All these lineages can be summarized within the two lineages of the Kama or oral transmission lineage and the Terma or "discovered dharma" lineage. These teachings have been transmitted through these two lineages in an unbroken manner up to the present time.

The transmission of the teachings from Garab Dorje until now is known as the individual oral transmission lineage. The oral transmission lineage is the way we receive teachings in the human world, while the mind-to-mind transmission lineage and the symbolic transmission lineage are in the dharmakaya and sambhogakaya. However, the oral transmission lineage is not separate from the mind-to-mind and symbolic transmission lineages—it embodies them.

The oral transmission lineage is also called the nirmanakaya lineage. For example, Guru Padmasambhava, Garab Dorje, Manjushrimitra, and all the Eight Great Vidyadharas are nirmanakaya buddhas. It is through the nirmanakaya buddhas that the teachings have come to us.

When the oral transmission lineage came to Tibet, it was transmitted through the Kama lineage, the Terma lineage, and the Pure Vision lineage. There are many great tertöns who revealed teachings about the practice of Dorje Phurba. One example is Ratna Lingpa, a famous tertön who discovered many Vajrakilaya teachings. Tsasum Lingpa also discovered extensive teachings on Vajrakilaya, and the text of this practice is the condensed sadhana that he discovered.

The terma teachings that Tsasum Lingpa revealed in southern Tibet contain some long lineage histories composed by the wisdom dakini Yeshe Tsogyal that were transcribed by Tsasum Lingpa. An example of how important and precious these teachings are for those who seek enlightenment is illustrated by Yeshe Tsogyal's words about the Vajrakilaya teachings:

> E MA, how wondrous! The combined practice of Vajrakilaya and Yangdag Heruka is the most essential practice you can receive. Vajrakilaya practice is the true path to enlightenment. It is a wish-fulfilling jewel; it fulfills all the practitioner's wishes. It is the wealth of every treasure. Vajrakilaya, the wish-fulfilling jewel, removes all obstacles. It is the great protector, it is the great treasure, and it is the great light.

> By practicing Vajrakilaya, you will achieve everything, so it is like a wish-fulfilling jewel. I myself, the noble lady, rely completely on Vajrakilaya, and through it I have achieved all my wishes. Since this practice is most precious, I honor and practice it. I am not going to keep it for myself only, but according to the wishes of Guru Padmasambhava, I am going to hide this teaching to be discovered for the sake of the many sentient beings.

NUB SANGYE YESHE RINPOCHE

This particular sadhana was discovered by the great tertön Tsasum Lingpa, who was a reincarnation of Nub Sangye Yeshe Rinpoche, one of the nine heartlike students of Guru Padmasambhava. According to Nyingma history, after Guru Padmasambhava came to Tibet there were three famous lineage holders, one of whom was Nub Sangye Yeshe Rinpoche. If we use the metaphor of a flowing river to describe the lineage teachings, then these three lineage holders were like three large reservoirs, holding and transferring the teachings in an unbroken way. The first one to hold all the teachings was Nyag Jnanakumara, who was also one of the twenty-five main students of Guru Padmasambhava. The second was Nub Sangye Yeshe Rinpoche, and the third was Zur Shakya Jungne.

Nub Sangye Yeshe Rinpoche was born in an aristocratic family of landowners during the reign of King Trisong Deutsen. At the age of seven, he met Guru Padmasambhava and received instructions from him, as well as from the famous master Shantarakshita. Sangye Yeshe Rinpoche was a genius, and because of his abilities he became a great master at a very young age.

When Sangye Yeshe was about twelve years old, King Trisong Deutsen invited a famous master from Nepal to Tibet. This master was Vasudhara, and he gave teachings to Sangye Yeshe. Ever since he was about seven years old, Sangye Yeshe had wanted to go to India, and after meeting Vasudhara he was even more inspired to travel to Nepal and India. At the age of thirteen Sangye Yeshe courageously set out for India by himself. He went first to Nepal and then to India, where he received many teachings from a famous master named Drushe Chetsen Che before returning to Tibet. In this way, Sangye Yeshe Rinpoche went back and forth to India seven times.

During his travels to India, Sangye Yeshe Rinpoche had many visions and realizations. He had previously received teachings from Guru Padmasambhava in Tibet, but he also miraculously saw Guru Padmasambhava on the border between Nepal and Tibet, as well as in the Cool Grove charnel ground. In that cemetery he also saw the famous dharmapala Mamo Ekadzati, who gave him secret teachings.

One particular vision of his occurred at Bodhgaya. While meditating in the great vajra *samadhi*, he saw a golden five-pointed vajra hovering one cubit above his head. The golden vajra descended to the level of his eyebrows, and he as tried to touch it, it jumped back up. That was a big surprise to Sangye Yeshe. When he resumed his meditation the vajra descended to the level of his eyebrows, but as he started to catch it, again it jumped out of his reach.

After that, he did a purification practice to refresh his meditation, developed more devotion toward the buddhas and lineage masters, and expanded his bodhichitta attitude for all sentient beings. Then he went back to the vajra samadhi meditation. This time, the vajra descended and stopped in the same place as before, and Sangye Yeshe was able to hold the tip of the vajra between his ring finger and thumb. As soon as he touched the vajra, it transformed into Vajrapani. At that moment, he actually saw the wisdom body of Vajrapani face to face, and received *abhishekas* and instructions from Vajrapani himself.

After receiving these teachings, Vajrapani gave him the Sanskrit name Buddha Jnana, which is Sangye Yeshe in Tibetan. Both mean "the wisdom of the buddhas." Guru Padmasambhava had previously given him the name Sangye Yeshe in Tibet, and in India Vajrapani gave him the very same name.

According to the Nyingma School, there are three inner tantras: Mahayoga, Anuyoga, and Atiyoga. After receiving the Anuyoga instructions and empowerments from many great masters, Sangye Yeshe Rinpoche translated and transmitted those teachings in Tibet, so he is considered the first Tibetan lineage holder of Anuyoga. In addition to being a great practitioner, he was a great scholar who wrote many books, which are still available in the Tengyur and the Nyingma Kama collections. Two of the most famous ones are a commentary on the Anuyoga teachings[34] and the *Lamp for the Eye of Meditation*.[35]

Sangye Yeshe Rinpoche is particularly connected with Yamantaka Heruka, the wrathful form of Manjushri, as well as with Vajrakilaya. He once showed a sign of his realization of Vajrakilaya by putting a wooden phurba into a solid mountain wall in a cave near Lhasa named Yangdzong Sheldrag, which is renowned as a site where Sangye Yeshe Rinpoche meditated for a long time. Pilgrims still visit that cave to see the hole marked by his wooden dagger.

Sangye Yeshe Rinpoche stayed in Tibet long after Guru Padmasambhava departed for the Glorious Copper-Colored Mountain,[36] and he had a very long lifespan of about 125 years. For example, he lived during the reigns of King Trisong Deutsen, Trisong Deutsen's son, and the anti-Buddhist king Langdarma who tried to completely remove Buddhism from Tibet by destroying the monasteries and retreat centers. Sangye Yeshe Rinpoche is renowned for saving the dharma in Tibet, particularly the tantric teachings.

Langdarma had heard about Sangye Yeshe Rinpoche and decided to summon him to his court. He said, "I hear you are a famous man. What kind of power do you have?" And Sangye Yeshe Rinpoche replied, "I have this kind of power," and he pointed his fingers in the subjugation mudra toward a rock mountain, which crumbled and fell into pieces. Then Sangye Yeshe Rinpoche said, "I also have this kind of power," and forming the subjugation mudra again, he emanated from his fingertips an iron scorpion the size of a yak, which was emitting flames and rolling his eyes. When the scorpion started coming toward the king, Langdarma quickly folded his hands and said, "From today onward I promise not to harm the Vajrayana teachings. You can leave now."

Sangye Yeshe Rinpoche lived for 125 years and then transformed into the wisdom rainbow body. He had many reincarnations who were born in Tibet and became great tertöns and scholars or meditation masters. Two of the most renowned reincarnations of Sangye Yeshe Rinpoche were Tsasum Lingpa and Mipham Rinpoche.

TSASUM LINGPA

Tsasum Lingpa lived during the seventeenth century, which was a particularly difficult period for Tibet. It seems as though Guru Padmasambhava wished him to live during this time because it was a crucial point in Tibetan history.

There were miraculous signs when Tsasum Lingpa was born, but he grew up as an ordinary person. He never stayed for a long time at any particular school or monastery; his knowledge and realization were attained through Dzogchen meditation. Tsasum Lingpa's lifestyle and character were that of a crazy wisdom yogi. He did not act like a normal person; instead his behavior was very crazy, as was his way of discovering the terma teachings.

Tsasum Lingpa is famous for recovering terma teachings from objects. He discovered termas within rocks and mountains, in the earth, and in rivers. He also discovered termas in old temples, in places such as ceilings and between the pillars and beams.

There are many stories about Tsasum Lingpa's life. A short outline about his life and how he discovered this Vajrakilaya sadhana is recounted here.

Tsasum Lingpa was born in Kham in eastern Tibet near the pilgrimage mountain of Jowo Zegyal.[37] His family was of humble means, and when he was conceived his parents experienced auspicious signs, which were sometimes a little wrathful and at other times very gentle and beautiful. This continued while his mother was pregnant, and when he was born there were powerful and wrathful signs. The family members thought there must be some spiritual influence connected with the child, and they invited both Bön and Buddhist priests to do protection ceremonies for the baby.

One day when Tsasum Lingpa was about six or seven years old, he went out with some hunters. They left him in a cave while they went on to the mountains to hunt. As soon as they left, a door opened inside the cave, and a red man with a harelip appeared. He said, "Oh, Sangye Yeshe Rinpoche, welcome! Please come in." He treated the boy very respectfully and led him through the door.

They went into what looked like a big house filled with many attendants. The red man was the lord of that family, and in the Tibetan style he arranged cushions for them to sit on to have tea and *tsampa*.[38] He was overjoyed to see Tsasum Lingpa and said, "I am so happy to see you; it has been such a long time. Until today I have struggled so much." But Tsasum Lingpa did not recognize him, and asked, "Who are you?" The man replied, "When you were Sangye Yeshe Rinpoche, I was your attendant and student.

We traveled together to India. When I was following you from Nepal to the Tibetan border, some robbers appeared. I fought with them, and they killed me. When I was dying I had a lot of negative thoughts and cursed them, and that brought me to this state. I have been through many changes in my lives, and now I am like this."

Tsasum Lingpa asked him, "Why do you have a harelip?" The man said that the harelip was the identifiable trait of his family, for he was part of the *Tsen* family of mountain spirits, one of the tribes of the invisible world. He had a harelip because it is the family trait of that type of spirit.

When the red man was saying all this, Tsasum Lingpa began to recover his old memories, as in a dream. They talked and had tea for a long time, until the man said, "Your friends are coming back! You need to be ready." As soon as Tsasum Lingpa went out of the door and back into the cave, the hunters came back. For Tsasum Lingpa this was a good experience, but it was mixed with feelings of sadness and loneliness.

When he arrived at home late that afternoon, his mother was very upset. She said, "Where have you been? From now on, you're not allowed to come inside the house," and that night she made him sleep outside the door. She said, "You are only six years old and already following the hunters. That means you are going to kill animals and others. Such a naughty boy! I do not want you to be like that, so I'm going to break your two feet with stones." She gave him harsh lectures and after that, for a month and a half, she hid his woolen boots so that he couldn't go out.

Around that time he started having visions of Guru Padmasambhava, wisdom dakini Yeshe Tsogyal, and other dakinis. He had many wonderful visions and dreams, and he started to talk about them and his experience with the harelipped man to his parents. But they did not believe him. They said, "Don't lie to us!" and did not want to listen to what he was saying.

During that time he also mentioned to his mother that he would like to join the monastery, but his mother said, "You don't know how to read. How you can join the monastery without even knowing the alphabet?" He kept saying that he wanted to learn to read, and finally his mother agreed that it would be a good idea and said that perhaps his uncle would agree to teach him. The next time his uncle came to their house, Tsasum Lingpa immediately said, "Uncle, please teach me how to read." His uncle said, "I will, but we don't have a chalkboard." In Tibet writing is usually practiced on chalkboards, so Tsasum Lingpa looked around the house and found a flat slate stone, which he brought to his uncle who said, "All right, we can use this." As soon as his uncle wrote the alphabet, Tsasum Lingpa was able to read it. His uncle wrote many other things on the slate stone, and in only one day Tsasum Lingpa learned everything he wrote down. His family was quite surprised to see how smart he was.

Once again, he insisted to his parents that he wanted to join the monastery, but they told him, "Oh, you don't know how to read well enough." He replied, "I know how to read quite well. Shall I read to you?" It was nighttime, and as there were only butter lamps in Tibet at that time, his parents could not see exactly what he was doing. He had only one page, but he pretended to read several pages of verses. He spontaneously composed a beautiful song, paying homage to Kuntuzangpo, then to Vajradhara, Guru Padmasambhava, and many great masters such as Tilopa, Marpa, and Milarepa. He tricked his parents so that they believed he was reading an entire text, and they agreed to take him to the monastery.

Tsasum Lingpa entered the monastery of Nang Chen Karda Gon in eastern Tibet. While he was there, a famous tertön named Tagsham Terchen was invited by the king of Nang Chen to visit and teach. The night before Tagsham Terchen arrived, Tsasum Lingpa had a dream in which a wrathful black lady appeared. She told him, "Tomorrow Tagsham is going to come to this area and give teachings. You must go and receive teachings from him. He was your dharma brother during the time of Guru Padmasambhava. You must remember this and go tomorrow to receive teachings from him."

The next day he planned to go, but when he saw some young monks playing in the playground who were not going to the teaching, he stayed and played with them. Tagsham Terchen taught for the following two days, but each day Tsasum Lingpa forgot to go. On the third night of the teachings, the black lady again appeared in his dream. She was more wrathful now, and she said, "I already asked you to go, but you haven't gone. Tomorrow you have to go, because the teaching is about me! You *must* receive that teaching."

The next day he went. The sponsor that day was the king of the area, and many dignitaries and high lamas were there. Tsasum Lingpa was just an ordinary young monk, so he was at the edge of the crowd. But people wanted him to move even farther back. He moved and was close to a meditation master named Könchog Tsering, who was known for being a very peaceful person. He thought Könchog Tsering would let him stay there, but Könchog Tsering got irritated at him and said, "Oh, you naughty young monk, you're disturbing my meditation practice. Go away!" And he pushed Tsasum Lingpa away.

At that distance and because there was such a big crowd, he could no longer see Tagsham, so he went behind the tent and listened from there. He couldn't see the teacher's face, but he heard almost all the teachings. But then someone saw him, and said it was improper for him to be back there, and told him he had to move again. When he heard this he felt upset and angry, and he just left.

He was so sad and angry that he lay down and went to sleep, and the lady appeared to him again, quite clearly. She was actually the wisdom dakini Yeshe Tsogyal, and she came down from the sky and consoled him like a mother would. She said, "You did well, you received all the teachings; you don't have to be sad." She showed him a lot of kindness and appreciation, and he woke up and went back to the monastery feeling joyful.

When Tsasum Lingpa was about seventeen years old, Lama Karda Chöje (the head abbot) and other administrators of the monastery found him to be very efficient and energetic, so they took him along as the head abbot's main attendant on a trip to central Tibet. Lama Karda Chöje was going to Lhasa to become the head abbot of Ganden Monastery, and many ceremonies would be involved.

While Tsasum Lingpa was in central Tibet, many of the monks as well as Lama Karda Chöje asked him to stay at Ganden Monastery and become a *geshe*, or great scholar. They encouraged him, saying that he was very smart and capable, and that he should remain there and study with them. He hesitated about making a decision, and one night in a dream Yeshe Tsogyal and many other dakinis appeared to him and said, "This is not the time for you to study. Instead, you must actualize the practice instructions that you have received. You have many things to discover and other responsibilities to fulfill." When he awoke the next day, he was totally decisive, and he left central Tibet.

He went on a pilgrimage to southern Tibet in the region of Lhodrag. One day while he was alone, he looked up in the sky and saw a thick white cloud in the southwest. He was feeling strong devotion to Guru Padmasambhava and Yeshe Tsogyal and all the other buddhas, and he was recalling some memories of his past life as Sangye Yeshe Rinpoche. His feelings of devotion were mixed with loneliness and sadness, and he began to cry and sing to that cloud. "You look glorious, like a snow lion standing in the southwest direction above this mountain. If you go further southwest, to the Glorious Copper-Colored Mountain, please give this message to my father Padmasambhava and my mother Yeshe Tsogyal. Now I am alone and wandering in the wilderness of the Tibetan land. Please come and help me." He composed a long, beautiful song, which he sang to the white cloud. After he finished the song, it looked like the cloud began to hurry over the mountain to the southwest.

That night Guru Padmasambhava and the wisdom dakini Yeshe Tsogyal, along with many dakas and dakinis, appeared to Tsasum Lingpa in a dream in order to console and reassure him. Guru Padmasambhava said, "Due to the habitual patterns of this life you have become obscured. We will purify these by bathing you. Then, we will give you initiation and instructions." After he was bathed, Tsasum Lingpa received teachings from them throughout the night. They told him, "It is due to your obscurations that you do not remember your past." In the morning he awoke with wisdom, having regained all his memories.

Tsasum Lingpa then returned to his native land in eastern Tibet. When he arrived at his monastery everyone said, "Now you have to take this responsibility and that responsibility." They all wanted him to take charge, and they put pressure on him. But during this same time, he was having visions of Guru Padmasambhava and the dharmapalas telling him what he needed to do. He tried to resign from the monastery, but it was very difficult because the monks kept insisting that he stay. So he stayed at the monastery for some time and fulfilled his responsibilities there, but in his heart he was preparing to leave as soon as the circumstances would allow in order to carry out the true purpose of his life.

The Key to Tsasum Lingpa's Termas

Tsasum Lingpa had many amazing dreams in which Guru Padmasambhava and the wisdom dakini Yeshe Tsogyal gave many teachings, empowerments, and transmissions. Many great dakinis of different colors also gave him teachings and instructions. Particularly, when he was nearly eighteen, he dreamt that Guru Padmasambhava and Yeshe Tsogyal told him that he would have begun to reveal terma teachings at around age fifteen, or even thirteen, but due to many obstacles and hindrances he was prevented from revealing them. They said, "Now you are approaching age eighteen, and if you are unable to reveal terma teachings within three years, all your missions of this life and future lifetimes could be jeopardized! Therefore, you have to be prepared and determined to carry on and change your life."

Guru Padmasambhava and Yeshe Tsogyal gave him many empowerments and teachings in this dream. They took him by the hand and pointed to a large storehouse filled with countless jewels and precious objects and said, "There are many treasures inside, choose one!" A lady appeared (who was actually a dakini), and they told him, "She will be your companion. You and she will undertake many beneficial activities. Today you must select the terma keys you would like to take from among these treasures." He asked, "How can I choose?" and the lady told him, "Choose the keys!" Tsasum Lingpa and the lady in the dream went into the storehouse, and he took a blue key made of sapphire. She told him to take another one, and he took a red key made of ruby. The lady took a white key made of silver.

When they returned, Yeshe Tsogyal smiled and looked at Guru Padmasambhava and said, "Our son chose the right keys!" Then Tsasum Lingpa asked, "What are these keys? What is their purpose?" They said, "The sapphire key is the key of all the oceanlike tantra teachings, the ruby key is the key of the voice of the Buddha's teaching, and the silver key is the key related to the skillful means of visualization, the creation-stage practice. These three keys symbolize the three kayas of the ultimate nature. If you had chosen the yellow key, you would have become very wealthy and powerful as a universal king, but you would have had many obstacles and distractions. If you had chosen the green key, it would have benefited yourself, but not others. Therefore, the keys you have chosen are good. Please keep them well protected." Then Guru Padmasambhava and Yeshe Tsogyal gave Tsasum Lingpa three small rolls of paper in red, white, and blue colors, telling him, "Keep these symbols of the three kayas close to you."

Guru Padmasambhava handed a dorje and *drilbu* (bell) to Tsasum Lingpa and said, "Keep these with you as well," and so he kept them with a lot of respect and prayed. He had been wearing multicolored thread on his ring finger, and he untied the thread and wrapped it around the three rolled papers that he received so that he could wear the three rolled papers on his ring finger. Then Guru Padmasambhava said, "Son, near the right side of the glacier mountain of Jowo Zegyal there is a mountain called Ahmye Mutri,[39] where you will see a rock that looks as though it is jumping up in the sky. In that rocky place, you will find special instructions about that ruby key that you took, which you must reveal before the fifteenth day of this month. You must go there very quickly—if you delay, you could miss that opportunity. Soon, after one year, I will send you another message with another invitation, but in the meantime, after you reveal this, you must travel far and wide, don't stay in one place." Tsasum Lingpa then bowed with great respect to Guru Rinpoche.

At that moment wisdom dakini Yeshe Tsogyal changed into an ordinary lady's form. She gave him other instructions and teachings, and then other ladies, some wrathful, some peaceful and beautiful, gave him numerous instructions and took him to wondrous places in this dream.

And at the end Yeshe Tsogyal said, "Now you go back and we will return to Udiyana, and soon we will meet again." In his dream Tsasum Lingpa asked, "If you don't accompany me, then who will accompany me?" Yeshe Tsogyal told him, "Don't worry, you will have soon an assistant. There is a place called Tashu, and there is an emanation of the wisdom dakini from Tashu who has all the characteristics of the *Ratna* family.[40] This dakini will await your arrival at the place where you are going due to your aspirations—your bodhichitta commitment. Later we will also come and help you." She and another dakini then flew up in the sky, and then Tsasum Lingpa woke up. He looked around and saw that the sun was already on the mountain's peak.

After that experience, he decided that the best way to be able to leave the monastery would be to act as if he were crazy. One day he dressed up in a strange fashion; he pulled his long skirt above his knees and put on a fox hat. He carried a thighbone trumpet and a long sword, even though it is forbidden to wear these things in the monastery. He came dancing into the courtyard, blowing his thighbone trumpet and making noises, such as "Ki, ki!" People stared at him; some people laughed, some got angry, and others just watched him. They all said, "Oh, he must have gone crazy." Then, he just danced out the gate.

Ahmye Mutri Mountain was two or three days away on foot, so Tsasum Lingpa set out to discover this terma. When he arrived at the mountain called Gyalmo Ri, he did not recognize that area, and he decided to stop there and rest, and perhaps have a dream, especially because he didn't know exactly where to go. So he went to sleep and that night he had a dream that the Zegyal Dharmapala along with all eight members of his retinue came to him in the dream. They said, "We have come to receive you." And Tsasum Lingpa asked, "Who are you, and what is your name? What direction should I go, and how far from here is the place where I should reveal that terma teaching? When will I arrive there? Please tell me!" And this dharmapala said, "My name is Zegyal Latsan Barwa, and I came here because of my previous commitment to you and Guru Rinpoche. Tomorrow, when you go from here, not so far from here, you will see a valley facing the northeast, and you should go in that direction. From there to the place where you are going to reveal the terma—there are three mountain passes that you have to cross. And, these days, there are many large gatherings there, and on the full-moon day, in the midst of the crowd, there will be a lady whose hair is tied up in a top-knot. You will meet that lady and speak to her, and she will tell you exactly where that place is. If you wait beyond the full-moon day, then the time will have passed; therefore, don't delay, go there directly!" The Zegyal Dharmapala made some offerings of food and other things, and disappeared in the sky.

Tsasum Lingpa awoke early the next morning, had tea, and immediately set out. Exactly as predicted in the dream, he saw a valley facing northeast. When he arrived, about a thousand people were gathered to circumambulate Ahmye Mutri Mountain. By then it was midday, so he securely hid his backpack and began searching for the woman the dharmapala had described in the dream, but could not find her. He returned to the place where he had hidden his small backpack.

Four women walked by, a mother and three daughters, who said they came from the Tashu village area. Among them, the youngest daughter had her hair tied up in a top-knot. She was very open and friendly, and immediately started talking to Tsasum Lingpa. He asked, "How old are you?" and she said, "I'm about sixteen years old." They all stayed together, and that evening he told them, "I am going to do Chöd practice," and he went to the mountain and did some Chöd practice in a solitary place. The next morning he returned and offered tea to the mother and youngest daughter, and asked the daughter many more questions. She always spoke beautifully and gave clear and perfect answers that he found to be auspicious. He asked, "What is your name? What family are you from? Where are you going?" She said, "I am the emanation of the Öser Chang,[41] and my name is Rigdzin Chi. I am not going to stay at home for a long time, I'm planning to go to Pema Kö."[42] He said, "I, too, will be going to Pema Kö, but not for six or seven years. You should also go to Pema Kö at that time, and we will meet."

Realizing that it was the day of the full moon, Tsasum Lingpa asked her to help him arrange auspicious circumstances right away. She replied, "Of course, I will make everything auspicious for you." And at that moment, he was confident that she was the woman in the dream. They made the Könchog Chidu[43] *tsok* offering of Guru Padmasambhava as well as torma offerings, and they distributed the tsok offerings to the many pilgrims gathered there. When night fell, he decided to go to the mountain again to do Chöd practice, so he told everyone he was going and walked to the mountain.

After climbing about halfway up the mountain, he encountered many howling jackals. They were moving toward him, and he was very scared, so he spontaneously sang Chöd prayers to Guru Padmasambhava and Yeshe Tsogyal. At the end of his song, he blew three times on the thighbone trumpet, and at that moment all the jackals stopped howling and went away. The moon was full and clear as he continued to climb the mountain.

Suddenly, Tsasum Lingpa saw a large man with blue-black skin and a lion face that filled the sky standing right in his path. He knew that this must be the Zhing Kyong Dharmapala, and he said, "Great Dharmapala, lead me on the path and show me the exact spot where I should reveal this terma teaching." At that moment, the dharmapala picked up Tsasum Lingpa, put him on the back of his horse, and took him for a brief ride in the air. As Tsasum Lingpa rode behind him, flames surrounded his body, and his face became very hot. The dharmapala's horse stopped, and after the Zhing Kyong Dharmapala dismounted, he picked up Tsasum Lingpa and dropped him on the ground. Tsasum Lingpa looked around, but couldn't see any mountains at all. Instead, he saw a fierce woman with a lion face whose long, fiery red hair filled the sky. This was the female dharmapala Singha Rama. From every pore of her body, red blood was sizzling, and in her hand she held a *khatvanga*.[44] It looked as though she was eating a whole human body, and next to her a lion and a tiger were roaring and growling.

Tsasum Lingpa was very scared and lost consciousness for a short time. When he awoke, fire was burning everywhere, and there were so many corpses on the ground that he couldn't go on, he couldn't even walk. Then, in an instant, he regained his awareness—he understood that this was an illusion, just like magic, and that not only this illusion, but all phenomena in the universe were illusory. He realized, "This emptiness illusion that I perceive is the display of my own awareness." The very instant he relaxed in the true nature of mind, the wrathful woman and all those visions were transformed. He found himself standing right in front of a big rocky mountain, and the female dharmapala appeared in her gentler, more peaceful, semiwrathful form. She opened a door in that rocky mountain, invited him to come in, and then lifted him up and pulled him inside. There he saw so many jewels, so many luxurious riches, and from them she picked up one small locket shaped like a sealed vase, made of a dark blue semiprecious stone.[45] The locket was the size of the length of the first thumb joint of a dakini. She had chosen that locket from among all those jewels and riches, and as she handed it to Tsasum Lingpa she told him, "This is what Guru Padmasambhava and Yeshe Tsogyal asked me to keep for you. Don't show it to anyone, and don't tell anyone about it. If you keep this a secret, it will open naturally, but if you tell anyone or show this to them, I will punish you, I won't be happy."

The female dharmapala picked him up again and dropped him at the foot of the rocky mountain. And when he looked up, she and the door in the mountain—all these appearances from before—had completely disappeared, like rainbows. The moon was still shining brightly, and all the surrounding mountains were white and sparkling. He didn't know which way to go, so he sat down and said prayers right in that place for a short time. He saw a deer sleeping there, and when she awoke and started to walk, he followed her for a short while. He arrived at a valley with large boulders and only two passages, but he didn't know which one to take, so he did prayers to the lama, asking where he should go. Suddenly, a small spiral of wind blew in one direction. Tsasum Lingpa thought this must be the right path and that perhaps it was the support of the dharmapalas. He took that passage and found the exact spot where he had met that lion-faced black dharmapala. From there he knew exactly where to go, and he went quickly down the mountain.

When he arrived in the valley, he felt a little scared, and he was very tired and thirsty. There was a spring with fresh water, so he stopped there to have some water. But when he drank, the water almost choked him, and he felt cold and a bit sad and lonely. He even felt like crying, but in the back of his mind he thought, "Why should I cry? I revealed the terma teaching, and if I cry it is not auspicious." Tsasum Lingpa didn't cry, but continued walking. There were many people, and he heard someone chanting the *mani* prayer, which made him very happy, and he shouted, "Ki, ki!" a few times, as is the custom in eastern Tibet. He arrived at his hiding place and found his backpack; all was intact inside, so he thought he would rest. But daylight was approaching, and he could not fall asleep. The sunlight was hitting the top of the mountain, and he wondered, "Do I still have that locket?" And he looked, and it was still there in his *chuba*. When he listened carefully, he could hear the sound of bees humming and also some beautiful music coming from the locket. He placed it on his forehead, throat, and heart centers, then kept it hidden inside his chuba.

And that is how Tsasum Lingpa revealed this terma key. Afterward, the mother and daughter saw him and asked if everything had gone well. They had tea together and made a fire puja offering before he continued on his journey.

Soon after that, Tsasum Lingpa went to Drikung Monastery in central Tibet, where he stayed for more than a year. He studied with Könchog Thinley Zangpo, who was his root teacher, and during that time he actualized the ultimate state in meditation. He also became famous as an expert on the practice of *tsa lung*, the ability to control the channels and wind energy in his body. For example, he could use his wind energy to travel great distances in a very short time.

After that he went to many different places and discovered many terma teachings. Also, during that time he had a vision of going to the pure land of Guru Padmasambhava, the Glorious Copper-Colored Mountain, and he stayed there for more than a month.

Generally, Tsasum Lingpa lived like a crazy wisdom yogi. He never stayed in one place for a long time gathering students, and he traveled alone. He discovered many terma teachings and ritual objects. The following story recounts how he discovered this Kilaya teaching.

Discovering the Dark Red Amulet Terma

One night while staying with a family in Lhasa, Tsasum Lingpa had a vision of a magnificent red dharmapala who was wearing armor and a helmet, and carrying a shield, a spear, and a sword. He was riding a large red horse in the midst of his retinue of seventeen attendants. This red dharmapala, who was the dharmapala of Vajrakilaya, said to Tsasum Lingpa, "Now it is the right time for you to go to Mön Sha'ug Taggo[46] to discover the phurba teachings. You must not delay." He also said, "You need an assistant. There is a dakini in Lhasa, an emanation of the wisdom dakini Yeshe Tsogyal, who must come with you. In Sha'ug Taggo there are many teachings that have been particularly dedicated to you by Guru Padmasambhava and Yeshe Tsogyal. You must go there now, and bring that lady with you."

Tsasum Lingpa told him, "I don't know any dakinis. I don't know anyone like that." The red man replied, "I will help you with her. Come to a certain spot tomorrow morning; I will assist you." The next morning Tsasum Lingpa walked to that spot, and as he looked down the road, he saw five girls walking toward him, and he thought that one of them must be the dakini. These girls were from aristocratic families of Lhasa, so they were very well dressed, and Tsasum Lingpa was a crazy yogi, so he looked kind of strange and poor. He was just standing there, and one of the girls paid a little attention to him, but the rest just kept walking. The one girl came toward him and asked, "Where are you from?"

Tsasum Lingpa said that he came from eastern Tibet, but he didn't know what to say next, and his thoughts became totally blank. Finally he said, "Could you show me the ring on your finger?" The young lady said, "Yes, I will," and she pulled off the ring and gave it to him. As soon as he held the ring, he became so excited that his wind energy made him leap far away. Instantly, he jumped such a great distance that he couldn't be seen. When he looked back, it seemed as though the ladies were looking toward him. But he was too far away to be sure.

He walked all day and reached a famous turquoise lake called Yardrog Gyumsto. When it became dark he lay down to sleep on the shore, and instantly the red dharmapala arrived with his retinue and said, "Good, you are here. But where is your assistant, the dakini?" Tsasum Lingpa said, "I didn't know who the dakini was." The red dharmapala exclaimed, "But I helped you! How can you say that?" The dharmapala became angry with Tsasum Lingpa and said, "You didn't do very well. I brought her to you." Then Tsasum Lingpa showed him the ring and said, "I do have this ring, but that's all I've got." The dharmapala replied, "You are not going to be very successful. The ring will help a little, but you must have a female assistant in order to discover the terma."

Tsasum Lingpa replied, "Well, I don't have a human dakini, but I will pray to the wisdom dakinis to help me." The next morning he prayed and prayed, and then he saw a white light, stretching out like a white scarf from a mountain in the Drikung area to where he was. In the midst of the white light the wisdom dakini and dharmapala Achi Chödrön appeared, riding upon a mule. She said, "You are calling upon all the dakinis. What kind of problem are you having now?" Tsasum Lingpa explained his problem, and she said, "Don't worry; I will help you."

She told him, "Ride behind me on the mule, and keep your eyes closed until I tell you to open them." He climbed on the mule's back and closed his eyes, and he felt as though they were flying through the sky. But he did as she asked and never opened his eyes. After a short time she said, "Now, we are coming down," and they arrived at Sha'ug Taggo, which ordinarily takes four days to reach.

The red dharmapala was already there, and he said, "Now you must discover the terma teaching in the center of this rock mountain. Guru Padmasambhava and Yeshe Tsogyal asked me to keep these teachings until you arrived. I have protected them, and now my job is done. They are your responsibility now. Take them."

Tsasum Lingpa climbed the rock mountain until he reached a spot that was blazing with fire. There he found a dark red locket that had insects crawling on it (the presence of the insects was a sign that it was almost too late to retrieve the teachings). Inside the locket were yellow scrolls containing the Vajrakilaya teachings. Along with the locket, he discovered a meteoric iron vajra, a statue of Guru Padmasambhava, and blessed relics.

When he pulled out these things, he looked around and saw that the sky was filled with rainbow light, and celestial music was playing. The red dharmapala was overjoyed. Laughing like thunder, he said to Tsasum Lingpa, "This time you did very well. I will continue to help the teachings and the practitioners of your lineage."

As Tsasum Lingpa looked around, he saw many doors cut into the rock, which were opening and closing. He could see many statues and terma teachings and other things behind the doors. But as soon as he would try to get those things, the doors would close. The red dharmapala told him, "Because you didn't get the right dakini, you are unable to take all of those things. However, you got the main thing, and that's enough for now."

Tsasum Lingpa was very famous for discovering termas from objects. When he discovered the Vajrakilaya teachings, he was alone except for several dharmapalas. But frequently when he discovered termas, he invited many students to accompany him. Sometimes three or four hundred people would go along. He would say, "At such and such a place and at such and such a time, I am going to discover terma teachings. Those who are interested to see how I discover them can come along." It seems as though he invited all of them because he was a crazy yogi; he would just invite everybody to come and watch him discover a terma.

This is how Tsasum Lingpa discovered the Vajrakilaya teachings, which were his main teachings at that time.

Great Heruka Vajrakilaya

CHAPTER 3

The Practice Text

THE READING TRANSMISSION

Before beginning the practice of Vajrakilaya, it is necessary to receive the reading transmission of the sadhana. This is very important because the words originated from Vajrakilaya himself. From Vajrakilaya they were transmitted to Guru Padmasambhava, from Guru Padmasambhava to the wisdom dakini Yeshe Tsogyal and Nub Sangye Yeshe Rinpoche, and from Guru Padmasambhava, Yeshe Tsogyal, and Sangye Yeshe Rinpoche to Tsasum Lingpa. This is the unbroken sound of the dharma, which has been transmitted in Tibetan.

The reading transmission is also important as the speech empowerment and as the continuation of an unbroken lineage. The power and blessings of the lineage have continued in an unbroken line from master to disciple until this time. These sounds carry the blessings and power of the lineage as well as the power of Vajrakilaya.

HISTORY OF THE TEXT

This text was revealed by Tsasum Lingpa, who was one of the 108 great tertöns. Although he is a famous tertön, many of his teachings have been very secret. In Tibet this text did not exist as a woodblock print; there were only handwritten copies. In 1960, when we arrived in India, we started looking for copies of Tsasum Lingpa's texts, but they were very hard to find. Since the open practice of Buddhism in Tibet had been destroyed, we thought that his teachings might have completely disappeared.

In India we were able to collect what would make about one volume of the twenty volumes of his terma teachings. That one volume was not complete, just pieces from many volumes. We did not have this particular sadhana. My father and I [*Khenchen Palden Sherab uses the first person in this chapter. –Ed.*] remembered it, and we wrote it down from memory, but we still did not have the introductory parts and the symbolic dakini letters. I kept looking for this sadhana, trying to find his texts in countries bordering Tibet such as Bhutan and Nepal. I continued searching for them, and in the 1970s I found this text in Sikkim, where I met a meditation master who had a complete version. I compared it with what we had transcribed from our memories, and it matched exactly, except for the missing introductory section and dakini script.

I was continually making inquiries, trying to find collections of Tsasum Lingpa's teachings. In the early 1980s I heard from one of my students, an abbot living in the city of Mysore in southern India. A student of his had come from Tibet with his family and had settled a long time ago in Assam, or Nagaland, in eastern India near the Burmese border. This young student mentioned that his family had a few volumes by Tsasum Lingpa. They were willing to send these volumes to me in New York—and one of them was a complete handwritten volume on the Vajrakilaya teachings.

When the volumes arrived, I copied and corrected the texts again and again because there were many grammatical mistakes. After much hard work, I was able to publish them around 1984. Then, when Tibet was opened to visitors, we asked many of our friends and other people there to help us collect Tsasum Lingpa's teachings. We gathered almost every volume and worked to publish eleven volumes, many of which we were able to send back to Tibet.

There is one more story about the publishing of this text. When I received the large volume of Vajrakilaya teachings from Assam, I found that the medium-length sadhana was missing. I made a great effort to find it, and sent many letters to Tibet. From eastern Tibet I received word of a man who had a copy of the medium-length sadhana. He had written it out in the style of a Western book during the Cultural Revolution. In Tibet the dharma texts, called *pechas*, have an elongated rectangular shape. The Chinese did not pay much attention to Western-style books because they did not seem to be religious texts. That man had copied the sadhana on Western-style paper and kept it on his person so that he could do the practice. He sent his text to me, and I was able to copy it and include it in the published volume of Vajrakilaya teachings.

LINE-BY-LINE COMMENTARY

The sadhanas presented in this commentary are the short and condensed versions from the large volume of the Vajrakilaya teachings of Tsasum Lingpa. The whole teaching is condensed within these sadhanas, which are entitled "The Coemergent Union of the Vajra Hero" and "The Practice of the HUNG of the Powerful Black Phurba."

This teaching came to us directly from Guru Padmasambhava and was written down by the wisdom dakini Yeshe Tsogyal and later transcribed by the great master Tsasum Lingpa. All three of them worked together, so these are not regular words but vajra words—enlightened words. These vajra words and syllables are words of wisdom that have power and bliss. The terma teachings are very special. Those who transcribe and transmit them are free from emotional defilements. All the buddhas reached enlightenment by following the true nature, and these are words of the true nature.

A practical and helpful method to explore the meaning and significance of all the aspects of this practice is to follow the text line by line.

Title

 བླ་མེད་ཡང་ཕུར་གའུ་དམར་ནག་ལས༔

LA ME YANG PHUR GA'U MAR NAG LE

From The Dark Red Amulet of Unsurpassable Yang-Phur

This text belongs to the Terma tradition. Among the Eight Herukas, Yangdag Heruka symbolizes the wisdom mind of all the buddhas, and Dorje Phurba symbolizes the activities of all the buddhas. Enlightened activities arise from the wisdom mind. When you reach the mind of the Buddha—when you discover the wisdom state—then enlightened activity is spontaneously there. For example, once buddhas have attained enlightenment, they turn the wheel of the dharma. According to Sutra Mahayana, Buddha Shakyamuni's attainment of enlightenment at Bodhgaya was the enlightened mind of Yangdag Heruka, and his turning of the three wheels of the dharma at Varanasi, Vulture's Peak, and Vaishali was the enlightened activity of Vajrakilaya.

This teaching combines the enlightened mind of Yangdag with the buddha activity of Phurba for the benefit of all beings. Naturally, this sadhana also contains the enlightened aspects of body, speech, and qualities. Having all five enlightened aspects of body, speech, mind, qualities, and action, this is the highest and most supreme teaching.

Gau is a Tibetan word that means "locket" or "amulet."[47] Here, the locket serves as a metaphor because its two sides are joined together: it symbolizes *dhatu* (the natural state) joined with *jnana* (wisdom). The *Coalescence of Sun and Moon*[48] is a tantra whose title is a similar metaphor of the union of jnana and dhatu.

The dark red color, *mar nag*, has two meanings. It is the color of our hearts, so it symbolizes something very dear, something quite special and secret. In a larger way, red symbolizes overpowering or magnetizing while black symbolizes action, and these are joined together. That means that our ego-clinging and concepts, which have been uncontrolled for many lifetimes, are going to be controlled, magnetized, and tamed.

The last word in the first line, *le*, means "from" or "within that." *The*

Dark Red Amulet of Unsurpassable Yang-Phur is the general name of the large volume of Vajrakilaya texts, as mentioned above. The next line is the name of this particular sadhana.

རོ་རྗེ་དཔའ་བོ་ལྷན་ཅིག་སྐྱེས་སྦྱོར་བཞུགས༔
DORJE PAWO LHEN CHIG CHE JOR ZHUG
The Coemergent Union of the Vajra Hero

Here, the vajra or *dorje* is a symbol of the absolute meaning or true nature. The vajra of the true nature is indestructible and unbreakable, yet it can destroy, penetrate, and subdue any other object. Since the vajra of absolute meaning is unshakable, it is also known as the primordial-awareness vajra. This vajra is like a daka or "hero," and its power is heroic because it goes beyond samsara and nirvana and beyond dualistic concepts to subdue all ego-clinging and habitual patterns.

Lhen chig che jor is translated roughly here as "coemergent union." This refers to your awareness, which is born with you, stays with you, and goes with you all the time. The primordial nature always accompanies your mind; they are never separate. As soon as your mind is there, primordial awareness is there. Although this is the case, people do not recognize the profound nature. Guru Padmasambhava remarked how strange or even shocking it is that people do not realize that wisdom is always there.

The word *jor* is generally translated as "remains," but actually it refers to the way you connect in order to realize the awareness that has been with you all the time. Through this technique you are making a connection or being introduced to the direct state of coemergent awareness.

The vajra hero who arises coemergently is the absolute Vajrakilaya. You have always had this absolute nature, and you have never been separated from it. This sadhana is a technique to directly introduce you to this primordial nature, using two methods: the visualization or creation stage and the dissolving or completion stage. Practicing these two stages will bring realization of the vajra hero, the absolute Vajrakilaya.

The title shows the meaning of the teaching, or what is contained in the teaching. By simply reading the title, you will understand what the practice is about. It is said that there are three ways a title can be read, which correspond to the level of the practitioner's ability. Those of the highest ability completely understand the meaning of the text as soon as they read the title, those of medium ability recognize in which section or group the text belongs, and those of the lowest ability at least know it is a teaching on Vajrakilaya.

The first syllable before the title, a long OM in Sanskrit, is the mark indicating the beginning. It symbolizes the five wisdoms and the five kayas.

At the beginning of the following line are some letters which are not Tibetan, but the symbolic dakini language. These five letters must be symbols of the five wisdoms or five kayas, but we do not know exactly what they mean; the dakini script is a very private language. It is said that tertöns who have exactly the same realization can understand each other's language or the symbolic dakini language. But otherwise, most people, even other tertöns, cannot read or do not know the meaning of those languages. The dakini script is amazing and very special.

This entire Vajrakilaya terma teaching was written in the symbolic dakini language by Guru Padmasambhava and the wisdom dakini Yeshe Tsogyal on yellow scrolls, and Tsasum Lingpa transcribed it into Tibetan. The original paper looks like ordinary rolled yellow paper, but people say that it cannot be burned by fire, and its ink cannot be dissolved by water.

Introductory Section

I prostrate to the Guru Bhagavat, Dorje Zhönu, and the hosts of deities.

The first line of the text is a praise that pays homage to Vajrakilaya. According to the Vajrayana, the lama is of the utmost importance. Having understood that Vajrakilaya (Dorje Zhönu) is identical to the vajra guru, Padmasambhava, we pay homage.

SAMAYA

The next line, "SAMAYA," is a reminder of the commitment involved in this practice. Following that are another four letters of symbolic dakini script.

I am a learned one from India. From the inner essence, the hero of coemergent union, I will teach the pith oral instructions of this profound and vast secret practice.

These lines give the history of how the text was hidden and for what purpose. "I am a learned one from India" is spoken by Guru Padmasambhava himself. The next lines indicate which teaching he is going to give, in this case, the pith instructions of Vajrakilaya. Even though this teaching is very condensed, it contains the essence of all of the ninety-five thousand Kilaya teachings; nothing is left out or missing. Here the word *men ngag* is translated as "pith instructions" and means something technical, important, and direct, through which one can easily discover the whole meaning. These pith instructions are a technique that Guru Padmasambhava taught for uncovering the entire meaning of the Kilaya tantras as well as the absolute Vajrakilaya state.

Sarasvati, Yeshe Tsogyal, retain this with your unforgetting wisdom. Write it down and conceal it as a precious terma.

The next line indicates to whom Guru Padmasambhava gave this profound teaching. The first holder of this profound lineage was the wisdom dakini Yeshe Tsogyal. If you are wondering who Yeshe Tsogyal is, this line describes her as none other than Sarasvati, the female buddha of wisdom. Sarasvati is none other than Tara, and if we go to a higher level, she is also Vajrayogini and Buddha Samantabhadri. They are all female displays of the same wisdom.

The dakini Yeshe Tsogyal has wisdom power. Guru Padmasambhava told her to use that power to hold these secret teachings within her unforgetting wisdom. And not only that, but to write them down in symbolic language and hide them for the future.

May a karmically connected heart son find this.

The last line of this section reads, "May a karmically connected heart son find this." This is known as the confirmation or seal to prevent this teaching from going to anyone other than the right person. It cannot be misused or wasted along the way before it reaches its destination. This seal is an aspiration that the text will go directly to the person who is going to reveal it.

The above lines also describe the transmission lineage of this text. According to the terma teachings, there are nine lineages, six lineages, and three lineages. Here the transmission is shown through the three lineages of the dakini lineage, the aspiration and initiation lineage, and the prophecy lineage. Guru Padmasambhava said that Sarasvati (Yeshe Tsogyal) must hold this teaching with her unforgetting wisdom, which shows that this teaching would be upheld by the secret wisdom dakinis. Without being spoiled or mixed up, it was kept in a secret way as the same fresh, perfect teaching. That is known as *khandro tegya*, or transferring the teaching to the secret state of the wisdom dakinis.

The line "May a karmically connected heart son find this" indicates transmission through the aspiration and initiation lineage. This means that Sangye Yeshe Rinpoche must be there to find the terma. The wisdom dakini Yeshe Tsogyal transcribed this in symbolic language and placed it in the locket. She and Guru Padmasambhava showed the symbolic letters to Sangye Yeshe Rinpoche, and gave their blessing and aspiration, saying, "This is your inheritance; this is the teaching to which you are connected. We dedicate it for you."

The third lineage transmission is the prediction or prophecy of who will reveal the teaching at a future time. At that same time, Guru Padmasambhava and Yeshe Tsogyal told Sangye Yeshe Rinpoche, "May you reveal this teaching." That is the prophecy. Having the three lineages—the dakini lineage, the aspiration and initiation lineage, and the prophecy lineage—makes this text one of the authentic secret teachings.

This sadhana is very condensed. Other larger texts contain more descriptions of how Guru Padmasambhava gave this teaching to Yeshe Tsogyal, how she transcribed it, and how they blessed it and made aspiration prayers for Sangye Yeshe Rinpoche. These things are explained in more detail in the other Vajrakilaya texts in this volume.

First are the customary preparations, the foundation of the practice.
Relax joyfully in a solitary place.

The following section explains the necessary arrangements and the shrine setup. The shrine is a very simple one, but when practitioners use the *samaya* substance, they should do so in the following way.

"Relax joyfully in a solitary place" means that while on retreat it is always important to be relaxed. Your mind, your body, and your speech must be relaxed, peaceful, and quiet.

Arrange the mandala of the vase platform on heaps of grain, and on top of that, place the victorious vase filled with substances and adorned with mouth ornaments, neck ribbons, and so forth, as described in the text.

Next, it describes the Vajrakilaya shrine. If you can choose the color for the cover of the shrine table, dark blue is best. If you do not have that color, it is okay. On top of the table, right in the center, place five small heaps of grain, with one heap in the middle and the others in the four directions around it. You can use grain or flowers. Above those put the mandala of Vajrakilaya, and on top of that put the vase.

If you do not have a representation of the mandala of Vajrakilaya, then the five groups of grain can symbolize that mandala. Above that, you must put the vase, which is called the "victorious vase."

If you have a choice of water to put in the vase, the best kind to use is unceasing water, which means water from a lake, spring, or river that has run continuously for a long time, and is very clean.

Then samaya substances are put in the vase water. The best kind is known as the twenty-five substances of the vase, or you can use *dütsi* or *mendrup*, which contain blessed objects. At the very least, the water should be colored with saffron.

The vase should be ornamented according to the tradition of the lineage instructions. The vase should have neck ribbons, which are usually of five colors or red, but you can use ribbons of either dark blue or red. Dark blue is the best. Kusha grass with peacock feathers is usually put above the mouth or top of the vase. If you cannot get kusha grass, then you should use leaves of a fruit tree, which means a tree that has no poison. Sometimes people use peacock feathers alone, but it is better to have kusha grass or leaves as well. One or two peacock feathers are enough; you do not need to use too many. If you have a picture of Vajrakilaya, you can put that above the vase, or with the feathers and kusha grass or leaves. However, if you cannot obtain all these things, then just having the victorious vase filled with samaya substances is enough.

If you can, it is also good to make a *torma*, a ritual offering cake made of tsampa. The torma and the vase are put in the center of the shrine. A small skull cup of *amrita* is placed on the left side, and a small skull cup of *rakta* on the right side. If you can do more, it is good to make other tormas such as the *cheto* torma, which is the commitment torma, and the *tenma* torma, which is a protection torma, as well as tormas for the other dharmapalas.

This text is short, so it says "and so forth," without mentioning all the things you can make.

Gather and arrange the feast offering, offering substances, and beautiful objects—whatever you have.

This line describes the rest of the offerings. Whatever you have available, such as the tsok ceremony offering, the seven kinds of offering bowls, and so forth, you should gather and display beautifully. If you cannot obtain all of these items—similar to the yogis who live in hermitages without many things—this is okay. It is not necessary to have them, but if you are able to get them, then you should arrange them beautifully.

Expel the obstructing spirits and visualize the protection circle. Having mentally blessed the offering substances, enter the mandala. SAMAYA

You can draw a cross or a *yungdrung* (a clockwise swastika) on the bottom of your cushion with white chalk or you can put a bunch of grains underneath your cushion. Then, sit facing the shrine.

Once you have displayed the offerings, even if you are not ready to do the main practice, it is important to bless the offerings. For example, after setting up the shrine, you may not start the main practice for another hour. But as soon as you display the offerings, you should say the offering blessing mantras, beginning with RAM YAM KHAM and extending through OM MAHA BHALINGTA . . . GUHYA SAMAYA, saying each mantra three times. If you are pressed for time, you can simply say RAM YAM KHAM and OM AH HUNG three times.

After making all the arrangements and sitting on your cushion, establish your pure correct motivation based on loving-kindness, compassion, and bodhichitta, as well as devotion. Then you can proceed to the actual practice.

Refuge and Bodhichitta

ན་མོཿ གདོད་ནས་ལྷུན་གྲུབ་གཉུག་མའི་རྩ་བ་གསུམཿ

NAMO DÖ NE LHÜN DRUB NYUG ME TSA WA SUM
NAMO The primordial, self-existing, innate three roots

ཀུན་ཏུ་རང་སེམས་མ་གཡོས་སྐྱབས་སུ་མཆིཿ

KÜN TU RANG SEM MA YÖ CHAB SU CHI
Are always, without wavering, one's own mind. Thus, I take refuge.

The first part of the practice is taking refuge. NAMO is a Sanskrit word that signifies "joyful body, joyful speech, and joyful mind." The sound of NAMO is an expression of your feeling great devotion and joy toward the objects of refuge.

These two lines express taking refuge from the absolute point of view. You are taking refuge in the primordially pure and spontaneous nature of the mind as being the innate three roots. The three roots—the guru, the yidam, and the dakinis and dharmapalas—are naturally inherent and primordially present as the nature of your mind.

This inherently accomplished primordial nature is the same as the coemergent vajra hero of the sadhana's title. Taking refuge in the primordial nature is the same as taking refuge in the vajra hero. Since the primordial nature is none other than Vajrakilaya and Guru Padmasambhava, this inherent primordial awareness is symbolized by the guru or Guru Padmasambhava.

Primordial awareness contains the qualities of wisdom, compassion, and loving-kindness, which are symbolized by the deity or yidam. By having compassion, loving-kindness, and wisdom, one performs beneficial activities from that awareness, and the activities are symbolized by the dakinis and dharmapalas. All the three roots are none other than the self-born awareness or the "coemergent vajra hero." This is the Dzogchen understanding of self-born wisdom.

The second line explains the manner in which we are taking refuge: we are always taking refuge in the primordial nature with an unwavering mind. This has nothing to do with a subject taking refuge in an object. This refuge is simply being in the natural state, without moving away from or going beyond that state. Maintaining one's awareness of the primordial nature all the time is the ultimate state of taking refuge.

ཧོཿ འཁོར་འདས་མཉམ་ཡང་ཕྱོགས་ལྷུང་བྱེ་བྲག་གནདཿ

HO KHOR DE NYAM YANG CHOG LHUNG JE DRAG NE
HO Samsara and nirvana are the same; one's perspective is the main difference.

ལེགས་པར་རྟོགས་པས་དེ་བཞིན་སེམས་བསྐྱེད་དོཿ

LEG PAR TOG PE DE ZHIN SEM CHE DO
Realizing this fully, I arouse bodhichitta.

The second aspect of the practice is arousing or developing bodhichitta, the thought of enlightenment or buddha mind. The reason we develop our bodhichitta is simply because primordial awareness or self-arising wisdom is there. Since it is there, we are inspired to develop the thought of enlightenment.

Everyone equally has self-born wisdom. There are no levels of high and low in relation to the primordial nature. It is not the case that buddhas such as Samantabhadra, Vajradhara, and Shakyamuni have good primordial awareness, and the primordial awareness of sentient beings is not so good. All of us are completely equal in having the wisdom nature. Therefore, there is no need to feel worried or sad. Instead, we can express our joy by reciting HO HO and HA HA, Sanskrit syllables which are expressions of great joy.

Khor de nyam means "the equality or sameness of samsara and nirvana," and *yang* means "even though," so the first part means, "even though samsara and nirvana are equal." Their equality is the ultimate view because both of them are merely perceptions or imaginary states of mind. When we realize that primordial wisdom is the nature of the mind, then that is nirvana. When we do not realize the nature of the mind, then that is samsara.

Chog lhung literally means "falling to one side," which can be translated as "bias" or "partiality." We become partial because we have not recognized the equality of samsara and nirvana; rather, we are inclined toward one side. *Je drag* means "to differentiate, or being able to separate," and *ne* means "the main point." The main thing that differentiates buddhas and sentient beings is that buddhas have the realization of equanimity, and sentient beings are biased toward samsara or nirvana. Having seen that the attitude of partiality is the cause of delusion, we generate bodhichitta.

The equality of samsara and nirvana is mentioned many times in the Buddha's teaching. Buddha Shakyamuni taught this very extensively in the Prajnaparamita teachings, the second turning of the wheel of dharma, describing 108 methods to bring clear realization of this equal state.

This teaching on equality was summarized in a special and simple way by the future buddha Maitreya, using eight methods that clearly show the meaning of equality. Also, the famous master Nagarjuna summarized the 108 Prajnaparamita teachings in a very clear and condensed way in the twenty-seven chapters of the *Mula Madhyamaka Karika* (*Root Verses of the Wisdom of the Middle Way*).[49] In this text, Nagarjuna used logical reasoning, which is a more intellectual or contemplative way to bring realization of the equanimity of samsara and nirvana.

Guru Padmasambhava summarized the teachings of both Sutra Mahayana and Tantra Mahayana, and along with other great Vajrayana masters he developed the Vajrayana techniques of the visualization and dissolving stages. These two stages, as practiced in the inner tantras, bring clear understanding of this equanimity. For example, from the Mahayoga point of view, the entire universe is a pure land—the totally awakened state. It is called the great self-born mandala. There is no need for any particular mandala, because the universe is primordially the mandala of realized beings; it is already the mandala of all the buddhas and deities. Meditating with that understanding brings the ultimate meaning of the Mahayoga tantra.

According to the Anuyoga tantra, not only does the external world exist as the mandala, but inwardly the body—the structure of our physical condition—is also a mandala. Each channel is already in the enlightened state; each movement of the winds in the body is the movement of primordial wisdom energy. Clearly understanding that the combined views of Mahayoga and Anuyoga bring enlightenment is the ultimate meaning of the Anuyoga teachings.

The Dzogchen teaching understands both of these states—the external and internal—to be none other than the display of self-born wisdom. Wisdom or primordial awareness is the source of every manifestation. Everything arises, exists, and dissolves within that state. Maintaining that state with clear understanding is the ultimate view of the Dzogchen or Atiyoga teachings.

In this way, samsara and nirvana are totally equal. There are no real separations or differentiations; it is only due to our partial understanding that we make distinctions. This attitude of partiality has made obstacles for us to attain our goal. If we realize the awareness nature and maintain it, that is known as buddhahood or enlightenment. If we do not realize the primordial nature and only look at one side, this creates the illusions of samsara. The notions of nirvana and samsara are simply a matter of knowing and not knowing. That was clearly taught in the famous Dzogchen prayer of Samantabhadra, the "Kuntuzangpo Mönlam."

The second line means, "By clearly understanding how samsara and nirvana are actually equal, and that I have made separations through partiality, I develop bodhichitta in order to bring great equanimity." This attitude is also expressed in the *Vairochana Perfect Enlightenment Tantra*,[50] which states, "All sentient beings, myself and others, from beginningless time are in the state of enlightenment. Understanding that clearly, I generate the mind of enlightenment."

Dispelling the Obstructing Spirits

After taking refuge and generating bodhichitta, the next stage in Vajrayana practice is the meditation to remove obstacles or send away the demonic forces. Usually, right before this section, there is a torma offering, sometimes known as the white torma offering, which is made to the local deities. Since this is a short sadhana, it is not mentioned here.

If we are going to send away the demonic forces, it is important to know what they are. Other tantric teachings of Guru Padmasambhava clearly state that the demonic forces are one's own ignorance. Ignorance is the biggest demon because ignorance is what gives rise to ego-clinging, emotional patterns, and mental concepts, which are like the retinue of the demon. Thus, the demonic forces are none other than one's own ignorance.

ཧཱུྃ༔ ང་ཉིད་ཡེ་ནས་རྡོ་རྗེ་གཞོན་ནུའི་སྐུ༔

HUNG NGA NYI YE NE DOR JE ZHÖN NÜ KU
HUNG Primordially, I am Dorje Zhönu,

Who is going to remove the demonic forces? The self-born vajra hero Vajrakilaya is going to subdue them or send them away.

In order to bring realization of the state of the vajra hero Vajrakilaya, this section begins with the syllable HUNG. HUNG is the direct method to invoke our inner wisdom or primordial awareness. This HUNG also symbolizes the five wisdoms and the five kayas. As soon as you recite HUNG, at that moment you clearly bring forth, with vajra pride, the absolute realization that you are the vajra hero Vajrakilaya. There is not the slightest hesitation or doubt about it. Instantly, you have vajra courage and vajra pride that primordially you are Vajrakilaya.

HUNG syllable
Calligraphy by
Khenchen Palden Sherab Rinpoche

ཕྲུགས་རྗེའི་རང་རྩལ་འགྱེད་པ་པོ་ནའི་ཚོགས༔

TUG JE RANG TSAL JE PA PO NYE TSOG
Emanating hosts of compassionate energy,

བར་མེད་ཁྱབ་པས་བགེགས་ཚོགས་མ་ལུས་ཀུན༔

BAR ME CHAB PE GEG TSOG MA LÜ KÜN
Who pervade everywhere and summon all obstructing spirits

ཨ་འཐས་གཞོམ་ཕྱིར་གཏོར་མ་ལེན་པར་ཁུག༔

A TE ZHOM CHIR TOR MA LEN PAR KHUG
To receive this torma, in order to destroy ego-clinging.

Many emanations come from the power of Vajrakilaya's compassion. Compassion is mingled with wisdom, and wisdom emanates in every direction, penetrating and summoning the retinue of obstructing spirits. This retinue is all the aspects of ignorance, such as ego-clinging and emotional patterns. In order to subdue and destroy clinging, they are summoned to the court of the wisdom of Vajrakilaya and asked to accept the ritual objects, the tormas. Torma has different meanings according to the level of teaching. This time, the torma is like a gift.

ཨོཾ་བཛྲ་ཏ་ཀི་ར་ཛ་ཧཱུྃ་ཛཿ

OM VAJRA TAKI RADZA HUNG DZA

གཉིས་འཛིན་རུ་ད་ཨ་ཀ་ར་ཁ་ཡ་ཛཿ

NYI DZIN RUDRA AH KARSHA YA DZA

The next two lines are Sanskrit mantras from the *Kilaya Tantra*.[51] Roughly translated, it is the command by the *döpe gyalpo*, "the vajra king of passion," for Rudra to come and take this torma. Rudra represents *nyidzin*, "dualistic concepts." Here the Tibetan words are included in the mantra to mean "Rudra, who embodies dualistic conceptions." AH KARSHA YA DZA is a Sanskrit mantra, which means that instantly, without postponing or making any excuses, at this very moment the retinue of dualistic clinging must come here.

ཧཱུྃཿ   སྙིང་རྗེའི་སྦྱིན་ཡུལ་མ་རིག་བགེགས་ཀྱི་ཚོགས༔

HUNG NYING JE JIN YÜL MA RIG GEG CHI TSOG
HUNG Hosts of deluded obstructing spirits, objects of compassionate generosity,

རྟོག་མེད་དེ་བཞིན་གཏོར་མས་ཚིམས་པར་དེངས༔

TOG ME DE ZHIN TOR ME TSIM PAR DENG
Be satisfied with this torma of nonconceptual suchness, and leave.

The next meditation is giving the torma to the retinues of ignorance and asking them to leave. This section also starts with HUNG because we continue the visualization of the primordial vajra state—Vajrakilaya.

The demons of ignorance are the object of compassionate generosity because ignorance is the exaggeration of things that do not really exist. Even though there is no existing ego, we cling to it; even though our mental fabrications do not really exist, we cling to them. The way we hold on so strongly has nothing to do with reality. So here, ignorance is the object of compassion.

The retinues of ignorance are summoned and given the torma of primordial wisdom, which transmutes every aspect of ignorance into wisdom. After the great transformation, they are asked to leave within the state of equanimity.

ཅི་སྟེ་མི་འགྲོ་ཞེན་པས་བཅིངས་སྲིད་ནཿ

CHI TE MI DRO ZHEN PE CHING SI NA
If, fettered by attachment, you refuse to go,

རིག་པ་རྡོ་རྗེའི་མཚོན་ཆར་དེས་གཞོམས་ཤིག

RIG PA DOR JE TSÖN CHAR DE ZHOM SHIG
You will be destroyed by the weapon of vajra awareness.

The first two lines of this section use the transformation technique gently and peacefully. If there is still strong clinging and attachment, then ignorance cannot be transmuted immediately. In these two lines, you invoke your hidden state as the vajra hero and deliver rough treatment, crushing dualistic concepts by your wisdom power. Arousing your hidden vajra wrathfulness, you destroy or smash ignorance into the dharmadhatu state.

According to the Vajrayana, this is exactly the same as the *trekchö* meditation of the Dzogchen teaching. Trekchö practice is to cut thoroughly all the emotional patterns and then include everything in the primordial nature. Using the weapon of vajra awareness is exactly the same as the practice of trekchö.

ཨོཾ་བཛྲ་བི་དྷོ་ཛྙ་ན་ཀུ་མ་ར་སརྦ་བི་གྷྣན་ཙིནྡྷ་ཙིནྡྷ་ཧཱུྃ་ཕཊཿ

OM VAJRA WIDHO JNANA KUMARA SARVA BIGHNEN
TSINDHA TSINDHA HUNG PHET

All the Sanskrit mantras in this text are adopted from the *Kilaya Tantra*. The mantras confirm the words that precede them. This mantra translates as follows: VAJRA is "indestructible," WIDHO is "awareness," JNANA is "wisdom," and KUMARA is "youthful." First, we have the youthful wisdom of vajra awareness. Then, SARVA is "all," BIGHNEN is "demons," TSINDHA is "cut thoroughly," HUNG is "wisdom," and PHET also means to "cut thoroughly." Thus, "The youthful wisdom of vajra awareness thoroughly cuts all demons." Of course, this mantra has many outer and inner levels of meaning; this is just the meaning of the mantra.

Now that we are free from being occupied by ignorance, we do not want to have any more relationship or communication with the demonic forces of concepts. Therefore, in the next stage we establish our defense.

Setting the Protection Boundary

ཧཱུྃ༔   རྡོ་རྗེ་གསུམ་གྱི་དཀྱིལ་འཁོར་བདག༔

HUNG DOR JE SUM JI CHIL KHOR DAG
HUNG The lord of the mandala of the three vajras

ཡེ་ནས་མ་བཅོས་གཞལ་ཡས་ཁང༔

YE NE MA CHÖ ZHAL YE KHANG
Resides in the primordially unfabricated palace.

རང་བཞིན་རླུང་ལྔས་སྲུང་བའི་གུར༔

RANG ZHIN LUNG NGE SUNG WE GUR
With the protection tent of the nature of the five winds,

སོ་འཐབ་འཐྲིགས་པས་མཚམས་ཆོད་ཅིག༔

SO TAB TRIG PE TSAM CHÖ CHIG
Densely intermeshed, close the boundary.

This is the protection-boundary meditation, as described in the first chapter.

Throughout every aspect of the practice, it is important to have a clear understanding of the state of the self-born vajra hero, which is also known as the perfect clear light state of Dzogchen. In order to maintain that understanding, this section of the meditation begins with HUNG.

Again, you need to invoke the hidden quality of vajra courage, so you recite, "The lord of the mandala of the three vajras resides in the primordially unfabricated palace," which means that your body is a vajra body, your speech is vajra speech, and your mind is vajra mind. Therefore, you are Vajrakilaya; there is no distinction between Vajrakilaya and yourself. There is no notion that the state of Vajrakilaya is something you plan to arrive at later; you are always in that primordial state.

At the same time that you embody Vajrakilaya, the place where you are is also naturally and primordially the palace or pure land of Vajrakilaya. This palace is not something newly created, but is naturally and since beginningless time a pure land. From the primordial state of yourself and this universe as Vajrakilaya, the five wind energies radiate.

The five wind energies, the *lung nga*, are actually the energies of the five wisdoms and the five elements. Wind is movement and change; it is the energy of the five wisdoms arising from the primordial state. The energy or power of the five wisdom winds becomes like a tent of protection, which completely surrounds this universe.

In general, wind is very important. This world, the earth, is based upon wind. Also, the wind element is the first active element when a child is conceived in the mother's womb. Conception is the process of the child's mind and wind element mingling with the parents' elements. At the present time, all our movements, our talking, our thinking, and our activities are combined with the karmic winds. Thus, the wind energy is very powerful.

Here, the five wisdom winds are radiating outward and appearing as five ritual objects: wheels, vajras, swords, clubs, and crossed vajras. Each type of weapon is one layer of the tent, without any space in between. The weapons are all moving very fast and continuously in every direction. The wheels are grinding and smashing, the vajras are moving back and forth, the clubs are beating, the swords are cutting, and so on, such that nothing can penetrate the tent of the five winds. The outside surface of the tent is covered with wisdom flames. This tent completely surrounds Vajrakilaya in every direction, cutting off all demons.

There are many, many weapons. It is useful to review the Tibetan in the fourth line word by word. The word *so* has many meanings; sometimes it means "teeth," sometimes it refers to the sharp point of a sword or spear; here it is the "sharp point." The word *tab* has two meanings: "fighting" or "grinding." Here it is used in the sense of grinding or meshing together. *Trigpe* means "heavy, strong, and deep." It is often used to refer to very thick clouds, so it also means "very dense." *Tsam* means "boundary," and *chö* means "stopping or cutting." That is the closing of the boundary.

The clubs are shaped like a stick with a bigger part, similar to a hammer, at the end. Hayagriva holds that kind of scepter. The five weapons are the scepters of the five wrathful deities. The five weapons and five winds correspond to the five wisdoms, the five dhyani buddhas, and the five wrathful deities.

The protection boundary is actually primordial wisdom. Primordial wisdom is loving-kindness, compassion, and bodhichitta. Here the five wisdoms are displayed as the five ritual objects completely encircling and protecting Vajrakilaya. This protection-wheel meditation has been taught many times in both the old and new schools of Tibetan Buddhism.

ཨོཾ་བཛྲ་ཏྲ་ཡ་མཎྜལ་ཡོ་པཉྩ་སཏྲ་བཛྲ་རཀྵ་ཡེ་སྭ་ཧཱ༔

OM VAJRA TRAYA MANDALA YAM PENYETSA
SARVA VAJRA RAKSHAYE SWAHA

This is a Sanskrit mantra from the *Supreme Awareness Tantra*. VAJRA is "indestructible," TRAYA is "three," and MANDALA is "mandala," so this refers to the mandala of the three vajras—vajra body, vajra speech, and vajra mind. YAM is the seed syllable symbolizing wind. PENYETSA means "five," SARVA means "all," VAJRA means "indestructible," RAKSHA means "protection," YE means "within," and SWAHA means "establishing."

This can be roughly translated as, "Establish the mandala of the three vajras within the indestructible protection of the five winds." You yourself are the three vajra states of Vajrakilaya, the entire universe is naturally the mandala of Vajrakilaya, and the five wisdom winds appear as protection; hence, vajra protection is completely established.

Blessing the Offerings

The following mantras are the blessing mantras for the offering objects.

RAM YAM KHAM

RAM is the seed syllable of fire, YAM is the seed syllable of wind, and KHAM is the seed syllable of water. These are seed syllables of primordial wisdom. The wisdom fire of RAM burns our impure dualistic concepts, which are scattered by the wisdom wind of YAM, and whatever is left over is completely cleansed by the wisdom water of KHAM.

OM AH HUNG

With OM AH HUNG, all impure things are completely transformed into the three vajra states of the buddhas. All appearances or forms are transformed into the body aspect of the buddhas, symbolized by a white OM. All sounds are transformed into the speech of the buddhas, symbolized by a red AH. All concepts are transformed into the mind of the buddhas, symbolized by a blue HUNG.

Each of these mantras should be recited three times. When you chant the mantras, try to relate to their meaning by understanding the purity of the symbolism. That is the way to practice according to the Vajrayana.

OM MAHA KALAKSHA PENYETSA AMRITA AH HUNG

The next line is the special mantra to bless the main vase, which is known here as the *namgyal bumpa*, the "victorious vase."

MAHA is "great," KALAKSHA is "vase," PENYETSA is "five," and AMRITA is the nectar symbolizing the five wisdoms. Together they mean that "the great vase is the five wisdoms." OM represents the body of all the buddhas, AH represents the speech of the all the buddhas, and HUNG represents the mind of all the buddhas. Since the mantra begins with OM and ends with AH HUNG, the vase is also the three kayas of the buddhas. Altogether, the victorious vase represents the mandala of Vajrakilaya and his entire retinue.

ཨོཾ་བཛྲ་པུཥྤེ་དྷཱུ་པེ་ཨཱ་ལོ་ཀེ་གནྡྷེ་ནེ་ཝི་ད་ཤབྡ་ཨཱཿཧཱུྃ༔

OM VAJRA PUSHPE DHUPE ALOKE GANDHE NAIVIDYA SHABDA AH HUNG

This line is the blessing mantra for the outer offerings: PUSHPE is "flower," DHUPE is "incense," ALOKE is "lamp," GANDHE is "scented water," NAIVIDYA is "food," and SHABDA is "sound."

The outer offerings are not just regular offerings; they are vajra offerings. Here we say "vajra" only once, since this mantra is recited in a condensed way, but generally "vajra" is said before each offering object: VAJRA PUSHPE, VAJRA DHUPE, VAJRA ALOKE, and so forth. These offerings have no impurity; they are beyond dualistic conceptions. In the Vajrayana, it is always necessary to understand the vajra nature. The understanding of purity, that samsara and nirvana are equal, means that everything is in the vajra nature.

The next three lines are the blessing mantras of the inner offerings of amrita, rakta, and torma.

ཨོཾ་སརྦ་པཉྩ་ཨ་མྲི་ཏ་ཧཱུྃ་ཧྲཱིཿཐཿ

OM SARVA PENYETSA AMRITA HUNG HRI THA

Amrita is sometimes known as medicine (*men* in Tibetan). The amrita offering represents all the liquids that bring life. Here we are offering the five kinds of liquid, or the five elements in liquid form, which are beyond death and beyond change. Amrita symbolizes all aspects of medicine or healing power. SARVA is "all," PENYETSA is "five," and AMRITA is "immortality." HUNG is the seed syllable for wisdom, HRI is the seed syllable for action, and THA stands for establishing or confirming that view.

ༀ་མ་ཧཱ་རཀྟ་ཛོ་ལ་མཎྜལ་ཧཱུྃ་ཧྲཱིཿཐཿ

OM MAHA RAKTA DZOLA MANDALA HUNG HRI THA

With the blessing mantra for the rakta offering, whatever exists in the form of red liquid or red color in the entire universe is symbolized by the rakta. MAHA is "great," RAKTA is "red," DZOLA is "glorious" or "flaming" or "erupting," and MANDALA is "mandala." We are offering everything in the universe that is flaming or erupting in red form and red color.

Generally, amrita and rakta are very profound subjects. There are many levels and ways to understand them. For example, amrita is like medicine, and medicine can be understood as the skillful-means aspect of all appearance. Rakta can mean the wisdom aspect of great emptiness. Another understanding is that amrita and rakta are like the white and red elements that unite when a child is conceived. There are many meanings for these profound, secret, and vast offerings.

ༀ་མ་ཧཱ་བྷ་ལིཾ་ཏེ་ཏེ་ཛོ་བྷ་ལིཾ་ཏ་བྷ་ལ་བྷ་ཏེ་གུ་ཧྱ་ས་མ་ཡ་ཧཱུྃ་ཧྲཱིཿཐཿ

OM MAHA BHALINGTA TEDZO BHALINGTA BHALA BHATE
GUHYA SAMAYA HUNG HRI THA

The third inner offering is the torma. MAHA means "great," BHALINGTA means "torma" (in both instances), TEDZO means "glorious," BHALA BHATE means "the mighty one and the powerful one," GUHYA means "secret," and SAMAYA refers to the samaya substances. This torma also has many different meanings, but basically, it symbolizes the union of emptiness and skillful means. So you are offering everything, whatever there is.

The three inner offerings are none other than the *tsa*, *lung*, and *thigle*—the channels, winds, and essence element. In a secret way, during this impure phase, the three inner offerings symbolize the three poisons.

Amrita is anger, rakta is attachment, and torma is ignorance. On a secret level, you are offering the three poisons.

The three inner offerings are very important. Their blessing mantras are part of the Vajrayana technique of instantly transforming everything into purity or wisdom.

The Main Visualization

Then, instantly recollect.

This begins the main part of the practice. This way of visualizing is known as the instantaneous style of visualization. According to the Dzogchen or Atiyoga teachings, there is no need to build up the visualization stage by stage, since everything is already enlightened. The enlightened state is revealed instantly, without having to go through different stages. "Then, instantly recollect" is just a reminder. At the moment you think of them, the mandala, the deity, and everything are complete. This is the way we are meditating on Vajrakilaya.

Visualization practice belongs primarily to the Mahayoga teachings. Even though this is an Atiyoga sadhana, it still has elements of the Mahayoga teachings. The three inner tantras are completely connected to each other. There is a Dzogchen tantra called *Dorje Sempa Nying Gi Melong Gyü,* or the *Mirror of the Heart of Vajrasattva,* which states that Mahayoga is the ground, Anuyoga is the path, and Atiyoga is the result.

ཧཱུྃ༔ སྟོང་པའི་ངང་ལས་སྣང་སྲིད་གཞལ་ཡས་ཁང༔

HUNG TONG PE NGANG LE NANG SI ZHAL YE KHANG
HUNG Within emptiness, apparent existence is the immeasurable palace.

Even in the Atiyoga system we have to know what we are going to visualize; thus, the first line of the main visualization means that the palace appears instantly from emptiness. Guru Padmasambhava taught that the purpose of chanting the visualization is simply to make it clear.

Again, we begin with HUNG, the seed syllable that symbolizes primordial awareness. Our meditation must be based throughout upon primordial wisdom.

To do this, according to the visualization style of the three inner tantras, it is important to know the three samadhis. The first is the true-nature samadhi, the second is the all-manifestation samadhi, and the third is the seed samadhi.

The true-nature samadhi is meditation on great emptiness, or the great true nature. According to the Dzogchen point of view, this is the view of trekchö. From that pure nature, clear light radiates, invoking compassion for all sentient beings. The second aspect is known as the all-manifestation samadhi. The combination of the first two samadhis is the third samadhi, the seed samadhi.

Here, the seed syllable HUNG is the seed samadhi. The first line shows both the true-nature samadhi and the all-manifestation samadhi. The Tibetan phrase, *tongpe ngang le*, "from the state of emptiness," shows the true-nature samadhi. The true nature is openness, flexibility, and manifestation. From great emptiness, without blockage or obstacle, the entire universe naturally arises as a great mandala. That is the all-manifestation samadhi.

Nangsi is the combination of two Tibetan words, *nangwa* and *sipa*. *Nangwa* is "the external world, the container," and *sipa* refers to the existence of the inner contents of the world, the existing sentient beings. *Nangsi* is translated as "phenomena and all possible appearances." Everything we see, both outwardly and inwardly, is already the mandala or the palace.

ཨེ་ལས་རབ་འཇིགས་པོ་བྲང་འབར་བའི་དབུས༔

E LE RAB JIG PO DRANG BAR WE U

From the syllable E arises the terrifying, blazing palace, which has in its center

འཁོར་ལོ་རྩིབས་བཞི་ཆོས་འབྱུང་ཏི་རའི་དབུས༔

KHOR LO TSIB ZHI CHÖ JUNG TI RE U

A wheel with four spokes; above that is the source of dharmas, then tiras.

From E, the single true nature, the frightening palace and the deities arise. E is the Sanskrit letter that symbolizes great emptiness, the source of all phenomena, the one great nature. E is the first letter of the Sanskrit word *eka*, which means "one." E symbolizes that everything has one nature. That is also known as the "one circle" or the "one *bindu*," which is the source of everything.

You do not need to visualize the syllable E; it is simply the symbol of the supreme wisdom body, the dharmadhatu, from which everything instantly arises. From that source comes the very frightening, blazing palace. In the center of the palace is a wheel with four spokes or four sharp blades. It is like a weapon the ninjas use; it looks like a throwing star. Above that is a triangular source of dharmas, a *chöjung*, dark blue in color. This triangle is like a thick, flat slab made of blue light. It symbolizes the whole universe.

Above the triangle is a vajra rock, and above the rock is a lotus with sun and moon disks on it. Lying on the disks are the *tiras*, upon which Vajrakilaya stands. *Tiras* is a Sanskrit word that refers to male and female demons, and also corpses. The male and female demons or corpses are above the dark blue triangle. You can visualize two demons, one male and one female, as representative of many tiras. They are lying side by side with their heads facing opposite directions. The male tira is lying face down, and the female tira is lying face up.

རང་ཉིད་དཔལ་ཆེན་རྡོ་རྗེ་གཞོན་ནུའི་སྐུ༔

RANG NYI PAL CHEN DOR JE ZHÖN NÜ KU
On that is oneself, Great Splendor Dorje Zhönu,

མཐིང་ནག་རྔམས་པ་ཞལ་གཅིག་ཕྱག་གཉིས་པ༔

TING NAG NGAM PA ZHAL CHIG CHAG NYI PA
Dark blue and awesome, with one face and two arms,

Above what we have been visualizing is the glorious Dorje Zhönu. His color is blue-black, he is mighty and powerful, and in this visualization Vajrakilaya has one face and two arms.

Vajrakilaya

ཕྱག་གཡས་རྡོ་རྗེ་གཡོན་པས་ཕུར་པ་བསྣམས༔

CHAG YE DOR JE YÖN PE PUR PA NAM

Holding a vajra in the right hand and a phurba in the left,

སྒྲོ་གཤོག་བརྐྱངས་ཤིང་དུར་ཁྲོད་ཆས་ཀྱིས་བརྒྱན༔

DRO SHOG JANG SHING DUR TRÖ CHE CHI JEN

With feathered wings extended, and adorned with cemetery ornaments,

His right hand holds a nine-pointed vajra, and he extends his right arm upward in the sky. His left hand holds a phurba, pointed downward. His vajra and phurba are made of meteoric iron and are sending out sparks of fire.

He has two wings; the right wing is made of vajras, and the left wing is made of precious stones. It is said that the right wing is the vajra wing, and the left wing is the precious wing. *Thangkas* (traditional Tibetan Buddhist paintings) usually depict the root of the right wing as slightly lighter and whiter, and the root of the left wing in different colors such as yellow or red. Vajrakilaya's wings are not like regular wings, but are fashioned like swords. Of course, these are all the display of wisdom.

Vajrakilaya is decorated with the eight kinds of cemetery ornaments. He wears a crown of five skulls and a garland of skulls. His upper garment is made of an elephant skin; at his waist, he wears a human skin; and his skirt is made of a tiger skin. He also wears ornaments of five kinds of snakes as his necklace, bracelets, anklets, and so on.

He has thick, long, dark yellow hair, which stands straight up and has flames coming out of each strand. On the top of his head is a five-pointed half vajra, which is also decorated with snakes.

A wisdom *garuda*[52] hovers above Vajrakilaya's head, emitting sparks of fire from every feather.

བརྐྱངས་བསྐུམ་ཞབས་ཀྱིས་དམ་སྲི་རུ་དྲ་མནན༔

CHANG KUM ZHAB CHI DAM SI RU DRA NEN
With one leg extended and the other slightly bent, crushing Rudra and corrupters of samaya.

He stands on one leg with the other slightly bent, as he crushes Rudra and samaya corrupters (these refer to the abovementioned tiras). His right leg is slightly extended, and his left leg is bent in the walking gesture. He is standing, ready to go, ready to act. He is on duty twenty-four hours a day.

You can visualize Vajrakilaya as being so big and gigantic that the three realms are like his cushion. And sometimes you can visualize him as being so small that his whole mandala can fit into a mustard seed. Any size is fine because Dorje Zhönu is very flexible.

འཁོར་ལོ་རྒྱས་འདེབས་གསང་ཡེ་པང་དུ་འཁྱུད༔

KHOR LO JE DEB SANG YE PANG DU CHÜ
He embraces Diptachakra, the secret wisdom consort, in his lap.

Vajrakilaya's consort, named Khorlo Gyedeb in Tibetan or Diptachakra in Sanskrit, is secret wisdom. She is light blue and has one face, two arms, two legs, and three eyes.

གྲི་ཐོད་མགུལ་འཁྱུད་ཞབས་གཉིས་སྐེད་ལ་འཁྲིལ༔

DRI TÖ GÜL CHÜ ZHAB NYI KE LA TRIL
Holding a hooked knife and skull cup, she embraces his neck and encircles his waist with her legs.

རུས་པའི་རྒྱན་ལྡན་བདེ་ཆེན་རྒྱས་པར་བསྒོམ༔

RÜ PE JEN DEN DE CHEN JE PAR GOM
She wears bone ornaments. Ever expanding is their great bliss.

The consort's right hand is extended toward the sky, holding a curved knife, and her left hand holds a skull cup filled with blood. She embraces the male deity's neck with her arms and his waist with her legs. She wears cemetery bone ornaments, like earrings, necklaces, and so forth, and a leopard-skin skirt. They are united in a state of intense bliss.

ཡབ་ཡུམ་སྐུ་ལ་འཇིགས་བྱེད་མེ་ཕུང་འཁྲིགས༔

YAB YUM KU LA JIG JE ME PUNG TRIG

The form of the father and consort is in a terrifying mass of flames.

ལོག་འདྲེན་བདུད་བཞི་ཚར་གཅོད་དཔའ་བོར་གསལ༔

LOG DREN DÜ ZHI TSAR CHÖ PA WOR SAL

Clearly visualize the hero destroying the four demons and those who lead beings astray.

The male and female deities are standing in a wisdom fire as immense as the fire at the end of the aeon. Clearly see the whole universe as the mandala of Vajrakilaya, very powerful and radiant, with wisdom flames moving in every direction.

This is our meditation. The purpose of this meditation is to invoke the power, energy, and realization of Vajrakilaya in order to destroy the four demons and misguidedness. Misguidedness includes all the concepts of sentient beings. You believe things to be true which are not true. You believe things are permanent, but they are always changing. You believe your ego exists and cling to it, but it does not actually exist. These are misguided conceptions.

As sentient beings, we move back and forth between extreme states all the time; we are never in the middle or the state of equanimity. We have notions that things are clean or dirty, permanent or impermanent, suffering or without suffering. We are either clinging to an ego and eternalism, or clinging to nonego and nihilism. These are all misconceptions.

Because of these extreme thoughts, we have trouble with the four demons. The four demons, or *düzhi* in Tibetan, are the demon of the aggregates, the demon of the emotions, the demon of death, and the demon of the gods. The first demon is clinging to the five aggregates—form, feeling, perception, formations, and consciousness. The five aggregates are subject to change, they are based upon impermanence, and yet we cling and hold on to them and never let go. That attitude is known as the demon of the aggregates.

Clinging to the aggregates causes the second demon, the demon of the emotions, to arise. By clinging to the five aggregates, we have the five emotions: attachment, anger, ignorance, jealousy, and pride. Also, by having the five aggregates, we have a sense that we will lose them. Because we are so strongly connected and so strongly attached to them, we are afraid that we will die and lose our five aggregates. This fearful thought is the third demon, the demon of death.

Because we have these different emotions and thought patterns, we never let our minds relax. We are constantly distracted by external things that we think are solid and necessary, and by being attached to small, sensory pleasures we end up with big problems. This state where the mind never has time to rest is the fourth demon, the demon of the gods.

Distractions are demons because they deceive you about your real goal. For example, you may try to do good actions, but one thing leads to another, and you think, "First I have to do this, next I have to do that," and you are always busy. The reason you have all these distractions is because you think that they're good. No one thinks God is bad; people always think that God is good, so the word "god" is used as a metaphor for what seems good. This is the demon of the gods.

The purpose of invoking Vajrakilaya is to subdue these four demons.

Symbolism of the Visualization

As for the symbolism of the main visualization, the wheel with four spokes symbolizes the four boundless meditations on love, compassion, joy, and equanimity. The *chöjung*, the "triangular source of dharmas," symbolizes the three doors of liberation. The three doors of liberation are that cause, effect, and their nature are all based on great emptiness.

The tiras have two meanings. First, as living male and female demons they symbolize anger and attachment. The male symbolizes anger and the female symbolizes attachment. Second, the tiras also symbolize corpses. That means that in order to attain enlightenment, it is necessary to go beyond the notions of dirty and clean. Ordinarily, we believe that corpses are dirty, so to break down our concepts of dirty and clean, Vajrakilaya stands on corpses.

Then, oneself is Vajrakilaya. His dark-blue color symbolizes the unchanging true nature, the dharmadhatu. One face means that there is one true nature. His three eyes show the actualization of the three kayas. The two arms symbolize skillful means and wisdom, and the two legs symbolize the two truths—relative truth and absolute truth.

His right hand holds a nine-pointed vajra which symbolizes that through the nine-yana teachings he liberates all sentient beings into the enlightened state. His left hand holds a phurba, the three-sided dagger that symbolizes that he liberates beings by the technique of the three doors of liberation.

The two wings extend gloriously on both sides. They show that Vajrakilaya is totally accomplished in skillful means and wisdom. He has no obstacles to benefiting sentient beings. He can fly everywhere and penetrate everything, so he is accomplished in both skillful means and wisdom.

The cemetery ornaments symbolize the action of breaking down dualistic notions such as dirty and clean and all the neurotic states. Being very wrathful symbolizes his compassion, and it is because of his compassion that he is cutting and smashing ego-clinging and dualistic concepts.

His secret-wisdom consort, Khorlo Gyedeb, is also known as Samantabhadri or Prajnaparamita. Their union symbolizes that Vajrakilaya is never separated from the profound true nature. Awareness and wisdom, or awareness and dhatu, are always together. Her curved knife symbolizes cutting off all neurotic states and ego-clinging, and her skull cup filled with blood symbolizes transmuting those into wisdom. Her six bone ornaments show that she is totally accomplished in the six paramitas, or that she embodies the paramitas.

The huge wisdom fire in which they stand symbolizes that these two deities are particularly dedicated to destroying all the darkness of ignorance.

Since this practice is very short and condensed, Vajrakilaya has one face and two arms. In the medium-length practice of Vajrakilaya, he has three faces, six arms, and four legs, with all the same decorations.

When Vajrakilaya has six arms, his first right hand holds a nine-pointed vajra, and his second right hand holds a five-pointed vajra. His first left hand is in the subjugation mudra, radiating flames. His second left hand holds a khatvanga (trident), which is emitting wisdom flames at its top. His two lowest hands, the third right hand and the third left hand, hold a phurba at the level of his heart. That phurba is as powerful as Mount Meru. In the elaborate meditation on Vajrakilaya, he has nine heads and eighteen arms. All these are the same Vajrakilaya, whether he has one face or three faces or nine faces. These are just different emanations or different aspects of Vajrakilaya.

ཨོཾ་བཛྲ་ཀཱི་ལི་ཀཱི་ལ་ཡ་སརྦ་བིགྷྣེན་ཏྲིག་ནེན་བཾ་ཧཱུྃ་ཕཊ྄༔

OM VAJRA KILI KILAYA SARVA BIGHNEN TRIGNEN BAM HUNG PHET

After the main visualization we recite the mantra of Vajrakilaya. This mantra invokes Vajrakilaya and confirms the meditation.

The words in the Vajrakilaya mantra include all his retinue and different emanations. For example, in the larger Vajrakilaya practice, in addition to the consort there are ten wrathful deities, four sons, and four gatekeepers. There are twenty-four dharmapalas (twelve male and twelve female) and another twenty-eight female wrathful deities, the *wangchug nyerje* (wangchug means "rich in power"). Not just one kind of power, but all kinds of power are embodied in these twenty-eight wrathful female deities. The mantra includes the retinue as well as the principal deities.

One word in this mantra, TRIGNEN, is not usually found in Vajrakilaya mantras. TRIGNEN or "nail" symbolizes that your meditation is held firmly. Your view and meditation are unshakable and unmovable;

they are maintained as one single state of primordial wisdom. TRIGNEN also refers to Yangdag Heruka. This phurba practice is a combination of Yangdag Heruka and Kilaya, and this part of the mantra symbolizes the unchanging wisdom mind of Yangdag Heruka.

Visualization Instructions

After the description of the main visualization, there are some instructions by Guru Padmasambhava for practicing this sadhana.

Visualize, emanate and gather, and so on, as is generally done.

Because this is a condensed sadhana, Guru Padmasambhava does not explain the visualization methods in detail. He mentions concentrating, radiating, gathering, and so on, as done in the other, larger sadhanas. For example, you can do the emanating and gathering practice while meditating on Vajrakilaya. To do this, visualize yourself as Vajrakilaya radiating wisdom light in every direction, and make offerings to the buddhas of the ten directions. That light invokes their blessings, and it returns and dissolves into your heart center. Then, once again you radiate wisdom light to every direction of the six realms, purifying the negativities and removing the obstacles of all sentient beings. That light brings out their enlightened qualities, their joyful and peaceful state, and then the light is gathered back into your heart center.

If you want to do the practice in a simple way, there is no need for offerings or an elaborate mandala, and so on.

If you want to practice in an unelaborated or unfabricated way, there is no need for any particular shrine or offering objects. Just do the meditation, and your concentration and visualization will be enough. Guru Padmasambhava mentioned this for wandering yogis and yoginis, as well as hermits, who cannot gather all the offerings. If you are meditating while staying alone in a cave, or wandering and meditating in different places, you do not need the shrine objects and offering objects—just do the practice.

If you want to do it elaborately, merely as relative skillful means, combine the preliminary sections with the concluding sections just like this.

For an auspicious arrangement, or if you just want to add small things, you can follow the entire practice as stated here. The preliminary sections mentioned in this line begin with refuge and bodhichitta, and go through the offering mantras. Later, after the main visualization, the concluding sections are the invitation to the *jnanasattvas*, the receiving of blessings, the dedication prayers, and so on. If you want to do all of these as an auspicious arrangement, then practice in this way.

Here, auspicious refers to the combination of positive causes and conditions. However, if you do not want to add all those fabrications, you can just do them mentally, and then directly begin the mantra recitation practice, so that you skip the preliminary and concluding sections.

Another abbreviation can be done when you are practicing this for an entire day. In the morning period you would do the entire sadhana, but in the afternoon period you wouldn't have to do the entire preliminary section. You could do the refuge and bodhichitta and then skip to the setting of the protection boundary, which begins with "HUNG The lord of the mandala of the three vajras." Sending away the obstructing spirits does not have to be repeated, because you already did that earlier, and you are in the same environment.

Invoking the Jnanasattvas

ཧཱུྃ༔ དམ་ཚིག་སེམས་དཔའི་ཐུགས་ཀའི་འོད་ཟེར་གྱིས༔

HUNG DAM TSIG SEM PE TUG KE Ö ZER JI
HUNG Light rays from the heart center of the samayasattva

ཡང་དག་ཡེ་ཤེས་དཔལ་ཆེན་ལྷ་ཚོགས་རྣམས༔

YANG DAG YE SHE PAL CHEN LHA TSOG NAM
Invite the perfectly pure jnanasattva, Great Splendor, and his entire retinue.

According to the Vajrayana, there are three *sattvas*: the *samayasattva*, the jnanasattva, and the *samadhisattva*. The meditator's self-visualization is the samayasattva, and the jnanasattva or wisdom deity is Vajrakilaya himself.

As for the samadhisattva, when practicing in an elaborate way, in Vajrakilaya's heart center you visualize Vajrasattva with his consort. In Vajrasattva's heart center is a blue five-pointed vajra marked with a blue HUNG. This is the samadhisattva or meditation sattva. When practicing in a simple way, the samadhisattva is the blue five-pointed vajra and the blue HUNG, without Vajrasattva.

Generally, of course, you are already Vajrakilaya; there is nothing else. However, on the relative level you are performing this in the pure land, so you invoke the wisdom Vajrakilaya to mingle with your meditated Vajrakilaya.

The meditation of inviting the jnanasattvas starts with HUNG. As the samayasattva Vajrakilaya, from your heart center you radiate five-colored wisdom light to every direction, invoking the blessings of Yangdag Heruka, glorious Vajrakilaya, and their retinues.

སྤྱན་དྲངས་ཛཿཧཱུྃ་བཾ་ཧོཿས་གཉིས་མེད་བསྟིམ༔

CHEN DRANG DZA HUNG BAM HO NYI ME TIM

With DZA HUNG BAM HO, they dissolve inseparably.

These two great wisdom beings, Yangdag Heruka and Vajrakilaya, dissolve inseparably into the samayasattva by means of four mantras: DZA, HUNG, BAM, and HO. The syllable DZA invokes them, and the syllable HUNG mingles or connects the jnanasattvas and samayasattva. BAM confirms and stabilizes that connection, and HO expresses joy and satisfaction with that.

These syllables are called the four mantras of the great gatekeepers, which are none other than the four boundless meditations. Each syllable also has a related symbol. DZA is love, which is like a hook; HUNG is compassion, which is like a lasso; BAM is joy, which is like a vajra chain; and HO is equanimity, which is like a bell.

As soon as you say this mantra, the jnanasattvas and samayasattva become inseparable, like water poured into water or milk poured into milk.

བདག་ལ་དབང་བསྐུར་བྱིན་བརླབས་བརྟན་པར་བཞུགས༔

DAG LA WANG KUR JIN LAB TEN PAR ZHUG

Please grant the empowerment and blessings, and stabilize them.

By doing this, you receive initiation and blessing, and request that your vajra body, vajra speech, and vajra mind will remain stable forever.

དུག་ལྔ་རྣམ་དག་ཕྱི་ནང་མཆོད་པ་འབུལ༔

DUG NGA NAM DAG CHI NANG CHÖ PA BÜL

I offer the fully purified five poisons and the outer and inner offerings.

Next is the offering of the five poisons, followed by the outer, inner, and secret offerings. The five poisons are ignorance, attachment, anger, jealousy, and pride. If you are unskillful, the five poisons are the extraordinary cause of delusion. But if you are skillful, according to the Vajrayana technique, the five poisons are the extraordinary source of great wisdom.

If you skillfully transform the five poisons, then they are the five wisdoms. Ignorance is transformed into dharmadhatu wisdom, anger into mirrorlike wisdom, attachment into discriminating awareness wisdom, pride into equanimity wisdom, and jealousy is transformed into all-accomplishing wisdom.

According to the Vajrayana, particularly according to Dzogchen, the five poisons are transmuted within their own state, without discarding or rejecting. In that way the five poisons are the great offering objects, the displays of great wisdom. There are no higher offerings than the skillfully transformed five poisons.

སྐུ་གསུང་ཐུགས་མཆོག་དངོས་གྲུབ་རྩལ་ཏུ་གསོལ༔

KU SUNG TUG CHOG NGÖ DRUB TSAL TU SÖL

Please bestow the supreme siddhi of body, speech, and mind.

By making the outer, inner, and secret offerings, you request Vajrakilaya to grant the supreme accomplishment of body, speech, and mind. You ask him to immediately grant the supreme accomplishment of the three vajra states—vajra body, vajra speech, and vajra mind—which is enlightenment.

ༀབཛྲ་ས་མ་ཡ་ཏིཥྛ་ལྷེན༔

OM VAJRA SAMAYA TISHTHA LHEN

OM has many meanings in the Sanskrit mantras, and here it means "auspicious." VAJRA SAMAYA means "indestructible samaya connection." TISHTHA LHEN is "remain firmly." This mantra means that the wisdom beings and the samaya being, or the jnanasattvas and samayasattva, must remain together firmly with a vajra connection.

ཨ་ཝེ་ཤ་ཡ་ཨ་བྷི་ཥིཉྩ་ཧཱུྃ༔

AVESHAYA ABHISHINYETSA HUNG

AVESHAYA is a Sanskrit mantra that means "invoking," and ABHI-SHINYETSA means "empowerment" or "abhisheka," and HUNG is like "insisting and requesting." This time HUNG is used to ask something urgently. You are insistently asking Vajrakilaya to grant the empowerment; you are invoking the abhisheka and blessings.

ༀབཛྲ་པུཥྤེ་དྷུ་པེ་ཨཱ་ལོ་ཀེ་གནྡྷེ་ནཻ་ཝི་ཏྱ་ཤབྡ་ཨཿཧཱུྃ༔

OM VAJRA PUSHPE DHUPE ALOKE GANDHE NAIVIDYA SHABDA AH HUNG

This is the mantra of the outer offerings, as described above. You are offering the best of whatever you can imagine, whatever you feel is excellent, all of the beautiful things that exist.

ༀ་སརྦ་པཉྩ་ཨ་མྲྀ་ཏ་རཀྟ་བྷ་ལིང་ཏ་ཁ་ཧི༔

OM SARVA PENYETSA AMRITA RAKTA BHALINGTA KHA HI

This is the condensed mantra for the inner offerings of amrita, rakta, and balingta or torma, as discussed above. The last word, KHA HI, means "enjoy," or "have a good appetite."

The Praise

In Buddhist verses of praise, we are praising the qualities of the enlightened beings. Praise has limitations according to those who do the praising. When their wisdom is limited, then the praise is limited. But the qualities of the enlightened beings are limitless, so our praise of the enlightened beings is a limited praise of the limitless state of enlightenment.

This is similar to what the famous master Chandrakirti spoke of in his *Madhyamakavatara*[53] (*Entering the Middle Way*): "When I praise the Buddha and then stop after a few lines, it does not mean that the Buddha does not have more qualities to praise, because his qualities are vast and limitless. It only means that my knowledge has reached its limit." He also gave the example of garudas or vultures flying in the sky, which finally have to land. This does not mean that the garudas have found the edge of space, but that they have to land because the power of their wings is limited.

Here Guru Padmasambhava praises Vajrakilaya in five ways. He praises Vajrakilaya's body, speech, mind, qualities, and action.

ཧཱུྃ༔ མ་བཅོས་ལྷུན་གྲུབ་རྡོ་རྗེ་གཞོན་ནུའི་དཔལ༔

HUNG MA CHÖ LHÜN DRUB DOR JE ZHÖN NÜ PAL
HUNG Unfabricated, spontaneous, glorious Dorje Zhönu,

The praise begins with HUNG, here symbolizing primordial wisdom. *Machö* means "unfabricated," and *lhündrub* means "spontaneously accomplished." Vajrakilaya is the uncreated and spontaneously accomplished one.

According to Dzogchen, from the point of view of the path, machö corresponds to the perfect view of trekchö, the view of "cutting thoroughly," and lhündrub corresponds to *tögal*, "leaping over." Machö is pure from the beginning, like the deep blue sky, and lhündrub is like the sun, radiating wisdom light. From the point of view of the fruition path, machö applies to the unfabricated dharmakaya, and lhündrub applies to the *rupakaya*. The rupakaya denotes the two form bodies, the sambhoga-kaya and the nirmanakaya.

The unfabricated and spontaneously accomplished one is Vajrakilaya, or Dorje Zhönu. As mentioned above, Dorje Zhönu is another name for Vajrakilaya; it is the Tibetan form of the Sanskrit name, Vajrakumara. *Vajra* or *dorje* means "indestructible," and *kumara* or *zhönu* means "very youthful." He is named Dorje Zhönu because he is the ultimate true nature. That state is beyond destruction and nondestruction, and free from birth, old age, sickness, and death. The ultimate true nature is indestructible and always youthful. The youthful vase body mentioned in other Dzogchen texts has the same meaning as *kumara* or *zhönu*.

The last word of this line is *pal*, which means "glorious." Being inde-structible and beyond death, old age, and sickness makes him the glorious one of both samsara and nirvana.

ཀུ་ཡེ་རྒྱན་རྫོགས་གར་དགུས་ས་གསུམ་གཡོ༔

KU YI JEN DZOG GAR GÜ SA SUM YO

Your body with the nine gestures, perfectly adorned, shakes the three grounds.

This line praises Vajrakilaya's body, which is completely decorated with the major and minor marks of a buddha and the eight cemetery orna-ments. These ornaments have symbolic meanings, as described above, and they are perfectly complete. *Gar* is translated as "gestures," but it specifically refers to dancing positions. Vajrakilaya's nine dance postures or gestures shake the three realms.

The nine postures are as follows. The first is *gegpa*, which means "very attractive, fancy, and rich looking." He is attractive because he has a lot of ornaments as well as the major and minor marks. The second gesture is called *pawa*, which means "heroic and very strong." Vajrakilaya has big muscles; he looks like a wrestler, like a strong, tough guy. He is heroic and powerful because he can subdue the four kinds of demons and all ego-clinging. The third gesture is called *jigsurung*, the "frightening gesture," because he emits flames, his three round eyes are rolling, his tongue is moving, his hair is standing up in the sky, and his body is very strong. This is the frightening posture.

The first three gestures are particularly related to his physical attributes, and the second three are related to his speech. The fourth gesture is called *göpa*, which means "laughing with sounds like thunder," laughing like HA HA and HUNG HUNG. The fifth gesture is *shepa*, which means "yelling." Vajrakilaya is yelling at ignorance. The sixth gesture is *dragshul*, which means "speaking very loudly with extremely wrathful sounds."

The last three gestures are related to his mind. The seventh gesture is *nyingje*, "compassion." Vajrakilaya is full of compassion and loving-kindness for all sentient beings without exception. The eighth gesture, *shiwa*, is peaceful. Even though outwardly he looks very wrathful, inwardly Vajrakilaya is the highest state of peacefulness; he is totally relaxed. The ninth gesture is *ngampa*, which means "full of excitement and longing." He always wants to help sentient beings. He never hesitates or delays; he is always ready to act for the benefit of beings.

By these nine gestures, Vajrakilaya shakes the three grounds or the three worlds. This does not mean he is like an earthquake, but he never allows the ignorance of sentient beings to remain settled. Through his compassion, he never lets ego-clinging relax. He is always shaking things up and raising everyone to the enlightened state.

གསུང་གི་ཧཱུྃ་སྐུལ་དྲག་སྔགས་འབྲུག་ལྟར་སྒྲོགས༔

SUNG GI HUNG DRE DRAG NGAG DRUG TAR DROG
Your speech, the wrathful mantra of HUNG, roars like thunder.

The third line is mainly praising the speech of Vajrakilaya, saying that his speech, the HUNG syllable, is the wrathful mantra sounding like thunder. His voice awakens ignorant sentient beings from the darkness of ignorance.

ཐུགས་མཆོག་མི་གཡོ་ཡང་དག་འཁོར་ལོའི་གཏེརཿ

TUG CHOG MI YO YANG DAG KHOR LÖ TER

Your mind, supreme and unshakable, is the treasure of the completely pure mandala.

The fourth line is mainly praising the mind of Vajrakilaya, saying that he has the supreme wisdom mind, unshakable by dualistic concepts. His mind is always mingled with the profound state of Yangdag Heruka. Vajrakilaya and Yangdag Heruka are like treasures that are in one single state, like one wheel or mandala that is never separated. As described above, this practice is a combination of these two deities, and on the relative level, Guru Padmasambhava fully accomplished the combined practice of Yangdag Heruka and Vajrakilaya at Yangleshöd in Nepal.

བདེ་ཆེན་རང་བཞིན་ཟུང་འཇུག་ཧེ་རུ་ཀཿ

DE CHEN RANG ZHIN ZUNG JUG HE RU KA

Union of great bliss and true nature, Heruka,

The fifth line is mainly praise to Vajrakilaya's quality of great blissfulness. Vajrakilaya is the great bliss, always in union with the true nature, the dharmadhatu. Skillful means is already united with wisdom. That is the quality of the Heruka.

འཇིགས་བྱེད་ཁྲོ་རྒྱལ་ཡབ་ཡུམ་སྐུ་ལ་བསྟོདཿ

JIG JE TRO JAL YAB YUM KU LA TÖ

I praise the form of the terrifying, wrathful, and victorious father and consort.

The last line praises the supreme buddha-activity of Vajrakilaya, which is to frighten ego-clinging, ignorance, and the five poisons. Both he and his consort have the quality of frightening the obstacles and obscurations, so Vajrakilaya is the king of the wrathful deities. Therefore, we offer praise.

The Mantra Recitation

ༀ་བཛྲ་ཀཱི་ལི་ཀཱི་ལ་ཡ་སརྦ་བིགྷྣན་ཏྲིག་ནན་བཱཾ་ཧཱུྃ་ཕཊ༔

OM VAJRA KILI KILAYA SARVA BIGHNEN TRIGNEN
BAM HUNG PHET

According to the general pattern of sadhana practice, after the praise comes the mantra recitation. When you are reciting the mantra, you should have the outer visualization all the time. Along with that, it is very important to have the samadhisattva visualization.

The larger Vajrakilaya sadhana states that while you are meditating on yourself as Vajrakilaya, in your heart center, a ball of light arises that is dark red or dark brown (the color of the heart) and has the shape and size of an egg. Inside that ball of light are a lotus seat and sun and moon disks, upon which Vajrasattva is sitting in the vajra posture with his consort.

In Vajrasattva's heart center there are sun and moon disks, and above that is a five-pointed blue vajra standing up. In the center of the vajra is a standing blue HUNG. Of course, all of these are made of light.

The HUNG is surrounded by the Vajrakilaya mantra, which is also blue and circles the HUNG in a clockwise direction. The HUNG is self-resounding, and each syllable of the mantra is also self-resounding. While concentrating your mind on this, recite the mantra, OM VAJRA KILI KILAYA SARVA BIGHNEN TRIGNEN BAM HUNG PHET.

When you recite mantras, it is important to give up the errors of mantra recitation. Do not recite too loudly or too softly, too quickly or too slowly, and do not omit syllables or add extra syllables. In other words, say mantras clearly, precisely, and at a reasonable speed.

The mantra is the speech as well as the mind of Vajrakilaya, so when you are reciting it and maintaining the meditative state, you are connecting yourself to vajra speech and vajra mind. You are already visualizing your body as Vajrakilaya, so you are within the state of the three vajras.

While you are reciting the mantra, it is good to concentrate on radiating wisdom light from the mantra circle in your heart, which purifies the world and all sentient beings. If that is too much to do, then it is also good to simply concentrate and recite the mantra.

When doing mantra recitation, if you have the qualities of good concentration, strong devotion, and great joyful effort, then there is no doubt that you are going to have signs of accomplishment. If your concentration, devotion, and joyful effort are disturbed by mundane thoughts and activities, they will not be pure, and thus you cannot expect quick results or signs. If you want to have good results in meditation, you need to have the good causes and conditions of concentration, devotion, and joyful effort.

As for the duration of the practice, it is good to practice for as long as you have time, according to your ability. No matter what amount of time you have, try to make your practice as pure and perfect as you can.

After the mantra recitation, according to how much time you have, you can insert the HUNG practice.

Dorje Zhönu

Practice of the HUNG Syllable

བྱ་མེད་ཡང་ཕུར་གྱི་ད་དམར་ནག་ལས༔

From The Dark Red Amulet of Unsurpassable Yang-Phur

སྟོབས་ལྡན་ཕུར་པ་ནག་པོའི་སྒྲུབ་བཤགས་སོ༔

The Practice of the HUNG of the Powerful Black Phurba

The HUNG practice is very important because the entire mantra of Vajrakilaya is condensed within it. The introductory section explains the power and importance of the HUNG practice. Then, there are particular times to do this practice. When you feel that somebody is cursing you, or that something negative is affecting you physically or affecting your environment or your vision, or when you are emotionally or psychologically upset, these are the particular times to do the HUNG practice. The HUNG practice will thoroughly cut all those things. It will destroy, pierce, and smash them, so this is a very powerful practice.

ཧཱུྃ་ཧཱུྃ་ཧཱུྃ༔

HUNG HUNG HUNG

The practice begins with three HUNG syllables which symbolize the three kayas: the dharmakaya, the sambhogakaya, and the nirmanakaya.

བདག་ཉིད་དཔལ་ཆེན་ཧེ་རུ་ཀ༔

DAG NYI PAL CHEN HE RU KA
I myself am Great Splendor Heruka.

འཇིགས་བྱེད་རྡོ་རྗེ་གཞོན་ནུའི་སྐུ༔

JIG JE DOR JE ZHÖN NÜ KU
The terrifying form of Dorje Zhönu

ཁམ་ནག་ཞལ་གསུམ་ཕྱག་དྲུག་པ༔

KHAM NAG ZHAL SUM CHAG DRUG PA

Is dark brown, with three faces and six arms,

ཁྲོ་གཏུམ་ཚ་ཚ་སྐར་ལྟར་འཕྲུགས༔

TRO TUM TSA TSA KAR TAR TRUG

And wrathful, dazzling with sparks like shooting stars.

Continue meditating that you are the heruka. This time Vajrakilaya's color is *kham nag*, which means "dark brown." He is very wrathful, emitting sparks like shooting stars. Here he has three faces and six arms. The central face is blue, the right face is white, and the left face is red.

གཡས་གཉིས་གནམ་ལྕགས་རྡོ་རྗེ་ཡིས༔

YE NYI NAM CHAG DOR JE YI

The two upper right hands hold vajras of meteoric iron,

མ་རུང་གདུག་པའི་བན་བོན་གཞོམ༔

MA RUNG DUG PE BEN BÖN ZHOM

Which destroy cruel and evil Buddhists and Bönpos.

His first two right hands hold vajras made of meteorites, or what Tibetans call "sky metal."[54] One is nine-pointed, the other is five-pointed, and they are flaming. Their purpose is stated in the second line: "to destroy the Buddhist and non-Buddhist cruel and evil ones." This actually applies to the curses and spells of black magic. Even though some people may claim to be Buddhists, still they may perform black magic or use the dharma or the Vajrayana in wrong ways. This applies also to non-Buddhists; whoever does black magic is destroyed by the power of these vajras. This does not mean that you are going to kill those people, only that their harmful attitude must be smashed or burned. Their negativity must be turned into love and compassion.

གཡོན་གཉིས་མེ་ཕུང་ཁཊྭང་གིས༔

YÖN NYI ME PUNG KHATVANG GI

The two upper left hands hold flames of fire and a khatvanga,

སྡེ་བརྒྱད་འབྱུང་པོའི་སྲོག་སྙིང་ཕྲལ༔

DE JE JUNG PÖ SOG NYING TRAL

Which cut off the life force of the eight classes of spirits.

The two upper left hands hold flames and a khatvanga, which tear apart live hearts of the eight classes of demons. The eight classes of demons are *gyalpo, tsen, lu, dza, sinpo, dü, shinje,* and *mamo.* They can also be classified as outer, inner, secret, and most secret demons.

མཐའ་གཉིས་རི་རབ་ཕུར་པ་ཡིས༔

TA NYI RI RAB PUR PA YI

The lowest two hands hold a mountainlike phurba,

རྒྱལ་བསེན་འགོང་པོ་དུལ་དུ་རློག༔

JAL SEN GONG PO DÜL DU LOG

Which crushes male and female samaya corrupters into dust.

Vajrakilaya's lowest right and left hands together hold a phurba that smashes or destroys the *gyaltsen,* the male and female demons (*gyal* is short for *gyalpo,* and *tsen* is short for *tsenmo*). Guru Padmasambhava mentioned that these two demons cause the most difficulties in these degenerate times. They are very active and disturb the emotional and psychological states of sentient beings, turning our mental states upside down and making us very uncomfortable.

The disturbance of the gyalpo is that your mind cannot relax. For example, even if you have everything you need, and everything is all right, still your mind cannot seem to relax and rest. This feeling that you are not happy and that you are not complete is the disturbing power of the gyalpo.

When you are not satisfied with anything, and want more and more, that is the disturbing power of the tsenmo. These two demons are very active in these degenerate times, and by turning the minds of sentient beings in wrong directions, they disturb the environment, cities, and entire countries.

Whenever the energy of the gyaltsen comes into sentient beings' minds, this restlessness becomes connected with anger, jealousy, and then attachment. These emotions become so active that people cannot rest; they feel that they always have to be doing something. When you feel this way, your speech, your mind, and your body all become completely restless. Vajrakilaya crushes the energy of the gyaltsen and instead brings happiness, harmony, and peace.

 སྦྲོ་ག་བཤོག་སྤུ་གྲི་བརྐྱངས་པ་ཡིས༔

DRO SHOG PU TRI JANG PA YI
The wings, like outstretched razor knives,

སྣང་སྲིད་ཀུན་གྱིས་ཚོ་འཕྲུལ་བཟློག༔

NANG SI KÜN JI CHO TRÜL DOG
Expel the magical display of all apparent existence.

Having outstretched, swordlike, feathered wings stops the manifestation or the delusion of all external phenomena. Simply thinking of extending these two wings will reverse or change the illusion of phenomena.

འཇིགས་པའི་དུར་ཁྲོད་ཆས་བརྒྱད་ཀྱིས༔

JIG PE DUR TRÖ CHE JE CHI
The eight terrifying charnel ground garments

ཡེ་ཤེས་འཇིག་རྟེན་ཟིལ་གྱིས་གནོན༔

YE SHE JIG TEN ZIL JI NÖN
Overpower wisdom beings and worldly beings.

The eight frightening cemetery garments, such as the elephant, leopard, and tiger skins, subdue the power or dim the glory of wisdom beings and worldly beings.

ལྟེ་བར་ཆུ་སྲིན་རྔམ་ཞལ་གྱིས༔

TE WAR CHU SIN NGAM ZHAL JI

The mouth of an awesome, powerful crocodile at the navel

དམ་སྲི་འདྲེ་གོད་སྙིང་ཁྲག་རོལ༔

DAM SI DRE GÖ NYING TRAG RÖL

Drinks the heart blood of the evil spirits who corrupt samaya.

At the navel center, a powerful crocodile consumes the heart blood of the wild demons of broken samayas. These demons refer to the negative thoughts of people who entered the path of enlightenment, but due to some obstacles or events fell back into worldly activities. The crocodile at the navel symbolizes removing their obstacles and transforming their negative states, and bringing them back to the path of enlightenment.

སྐུ་སྨད་གནས་ལྕགས་ཕུར་གཞམ་གྱིས༔

KU ME NAM CHAG PUR SHAM JI

The lower body, shaped like the blade of a meteoric iron phurba,

སྟོང་ཁམས་རུ་དྲའི་སྲོག་དབུགས་ཕྲལ༔

TONG KHAM RU DRE SOG UG TRAL

Cuts off the life breath of the rudras of the three realms.

In this sadhana, Vajrakilaya's lower body is shaped like the three pointed blades of a phurba. The ritual-object phurba has a crocodile mouth at the navel, and the lower part is made of a meteorite. It destroys all clinging to an ego as well as to the entire universe. Here "rudras" refers to the biggest demons of all—ignorance and ego-clinging. These are the giant demons that you must destroy.

སྐུ་ལ་མེ་ཕུང་འཁྲིགས་པ་ཡིས༔

KU LA ME PUNG TRIG PA YI

Around the body, a mass of flames

ལོག་འདྲེན་བདུད་བཞིའི་དཔུང་ཚོགས་བསྲེགས༔

LOG DREN DÜ ZHI PUNG TSOG SEG

Burns the troops of the four demons and those who lead beings astray.

The fire consumes the four demons. These are the same four demons discussed above: the demons of the aggregates, the emotions, death, and the gods.

ཡུམ་ཆེན་འཁོར་ལོ་རྒྱས་འདེབས་འཁྲིལ༔

YUM CHEN KHOR LO JE DEB TRIL

Embracing the great mother, Diptachakra,

The great mother or the consort, the female buddha, Diptachakra, is embracing Vajrakilaya.

ཁྲོ་རྒྱལ་སྟོབས་ལྡན་ཀཱི་ལ་ཡ༔

TRO JAL TOB DEN KILAYA

The wrathful king, powerful Kilaya,

བདུད་འདུལ་དཔལ་གྱི་སྐུ་རུ་ཤར༔

DÜ DÜL PAL JI KU RU SHAR

Appears in a glorious form that subdues demons.

The wrathful, powerful king, Vajrakilaya, arises with the glory of both samsara and nirvana in order to subdue all negativities.

དབང་སྡུད་ཟིལ་གནོན་ལྷུན་གྱིས་གྲུབ༔

WANG DÜ ZIL NÖN LHÜN JI DRUB

With the power of subjugation, spontaneously overwhelming,

བདུད་དགྲ་ཚར་གཅོད་ལས་གྲུབ་གྱུརཿ

DÜ DRA TSAR CHÖ LE DRUB JUR

The action of annihilating hostile demons is accomplished.

By meditating on these two powerful deities, Vajrakilaya and Dipta-chakra, the subjugation of all obstacles is naturally accomplished. As soon as you are able to subdue your ego-clinging, when you are able to over-power your own perceptions and conceptions, at that moment "all power of subjugation is spontaneously accomplished."

You need to apply this subjugation to your own inner state—to your own ego-clinging, ignorance, attachment, anger, and so forth. That is what you need to smash and transform. It is not necessary to look outside your-self for the demons; this is not something that you are doing to others. When you meditate on Vajrakilaya, if you think you have to cut down or smash someone else or something external, that is misguided and a wrong practice of the Vajrayana teachings. If you think you have to do that to others, perhaps you will soon become a demon, like Rudra, yourself.

When you are able to destroy all demons and harmful obstacles, then you are naturally accomplished, and you maintain the wisdom power of Vajrakilaya by subduing your own ego-clinging. If you can do that, then naturally you will be able to help all sentient beings.

ཧཱུྃ་ཧཱུྃ་ཧཱུྃཿ

HUNG HUNG HUNG

ཧཱུྃ་ཧཱུྃ་ཧཱུྃཿ

HUNG HUNG HUNG

ཧཱུྃ་ཧཱུྃ་ཧཱུྃ་ཧཱུྃཿ

HUNG HUNG HUNG HUNG

After chanting the visualization, remain in the great sound-emptiness and recite the HUNG mantra for as long as you have time. When chanting the triple HUNG, at first you say them as three distinct syllables. Do that for a short time, and then merge the HUNGs into one sound. Mentally you may be chanting separate HUNGs, but what you hear is like one continuous tune. At this point in the sadhana ten HUNGs are given, but that is merely symbolic of the ten herukas who are the retinue or emanations of Vajrakilaya.

Chanting the HUNG is a very powerful practice. HUNG can be meditated upon in many different forms; HUNG symbolizes Vajrakilaya himself, the ritual objects, and primordial wisdom. HUNG is very important.

When you do not have much time, you can do the HUNG practice by itself. Or another short form would be to meditate on Vajrakilaya for a short time, even by simply reciting the mantra OM VAJRA KILI KILAYA SARVA BIGHNEN TRIGNEN BAM HUNG PHET, and then do a short HUNG practice. If you have already done the HUNG practice many times and know its visualization and style, you can immediately invoke that form of Vajrakilaya and chant the triple HUNG mantra for as long as you have time. Blessings are conferred that way as well. Of course, if you have time, do the entire practice as described here.

Amending Errors in the Mantra Recitation

After reciting the HUNG mantra, or the long Vajrakilaya mantra if you are not doing the HUNG practice, recite the Sanskrit vowels and consonants, the Vajrasattva mantra, and the interdependent co-origination mantra three times each. We recite the vowels and consonants in order to fill in the gaps and remove any errors connected with the words of the mantra recitation. Reciting the Vajrasattva mantra removes any errors connected with your meditation or concentration, and reciting the mantra of interdependent co-origination confirms the power of the mantra. Since everything is dependent upon everything else, the power of meditation and recitation is also interdependent.

Receiving the Empowerments

ཧཱུྃ༔ གདོད་ནས་ལྷུན་སྐྱེས་རྡོ་རྗེ་གཞོན་ནུའི་སྐུ༔

HUNG DÖ NE LHEN CHE DOR JE ZHÖN NÜ KU

HUNG The form of Dorje Zhönu, primordially coemergent,

ལྔ་ལྡན་ཡེ་ཤེས་བྱིན་རླབས་ནུས་མཐུ་ཡིས༔

NGA DEN YE SHE JIN LAB NÜ TU YI

Has the power to confer the blessings of the five wisdoms.

སྐལ་ལྡན་བདག་ལ་དབང་བསྐུར་རྒྱུད་སྨིན་ཏེ༔

KAL DEN DAG LA WANG KUR JÜ MIN TE

Please empower me, a fortunate one, and ripen my being.

མཆོག་ཐུན་འབྲས་བུ་ཡོངས་རྫོགས་དངོས་གྲུབ་སྩོལ༔

CHOG TÜN DRE BU YONG DZOG NGÖ DRUB TSÖL

Grant the complete fruition of the ordinary and supreme siddhis.

After that, you return to the first sadhana and do the practice of "Receiving the Empowerments." At this point you receive the blessings and do the practice of the completion stage.

To receive the empowerments, you start with the HUNG syllable while continuing to visualize yourself as Vajrakilaya. At the moment you say HUNG, the samadhisattva in your heart center radiates light to create a jnanasattva Vajrakilaya right in front of you. Remain as Vajrakilaya, and in the sky in front of you there is another Vajrakilaya. That jnanasattva Vajrakilaya radiates five-colored wisdom light back to you, which confers the blessings of the five wisdoms. Although you are none other than Vajrakilaya, you receive blessings through that wisdom light returning to you.

To visualize this in more detail, from the forehead, speech, and heart centers of the wisdom Vajrakilaya, white, red, and blue light radiates to your three centers. Finally, five-colored light again radiates from his heart center and enters your heart center. In this way you receive the four empowerments.

ཨོཾ་བཛྲ་ཀུ་མ་ར་བྃ་ཌཱ་ཀི་ནི་ཧཱུྃ༔

OM VAJRA KUMARA BAM DAKINI HUNG

Both Vajrakilaya and his consort, Diptachakra, confer these empower-ments. In the Sanskrit mantra, VAJRA KUMARA refers to Vajrakilaya, and BAM DAKINI to the consort. Visualize that you are receiving blessings from both of them.

ཀཱ་ཡ་ཝཱ་ཀ་ཙིཏྟ་སིདྡྷི་ཧཱུྃ༔

KAYA WAKA TSITTA SIDDHI HUNG

KAYA is the body blessing, WAKA is the speech blessing, TSITTA is the mind blessing, and SIDDHI blesses all three—body, speech, and mind. At the end of this mantra, when you say HUNG, the Vajrakilaya in front of you dissolves back into your heart center.

By receiving these blessings and empowerments, the ordinary and extraordinary siddhis are granted and accomplished immediately.

The Completion Stage

After that, dissolve the visualization. This is called the completion stage. Having the visualization of Vajrakilaya as before, you say HUNG as a reminder of that whole visualization. Then the entire visualization dissolves into the mandala of primordial wisdom or the *kadag* state.

ཧཱུྃ༔ མི་དམིགས་དཀྱིལ་འཁོར་ཀ་དག་དབྱིངས༔

HUNG MI MIG CHIL KHOR KA DAG YING

HUNG Dissolve into the perfectly pure space, the mandala beyond thought,

There are different ways to dissolve the visualization. The direct approach is to simply merge with the natural state, or immediately transform every-thing into the state of primordial wisdom. It is perfectly fine to do it this way.

Or if you prefer to dissolve the visualization in a graduated and elaborate way, then you begin by dissolving the entire universe, the pure land of Sangchen Meri Barwa, into the retinue of Vajrakilaya. The retinue dissolves into the consort, and the consort dissolves into Vajrakilaya. Then, from his cushion or throne, Vajrakilaya's body dissolves into the HUNG syllable in his heart center. The HUNG dissolves from the bottom to the top, and then into the dharmakaya. This is the meditation to "dissolve into the perfectly pure space, the mandala beyond thought." You can do the dissolving of the visualization whichever way you like.

རང་བཞིན་ཡེ་ཤེས་ཀློང་དུ་ཧོ༔

RANG ZHIN YE SHE LONG DU HO
The vast expanse of self-existing wisdom. HO!

Whichever visualization you do of the elaborate, frightening, and mighty deity is simply a display of primordial wisdom. This entire system arises from primordial wisdom, is maintained within the activities and display of primordial wisdom, and completely dissolves back into primordial wisdom.

The visualization is dissolved into the primordial nature, which is the basic ground of all phenomena, or the basic ground of Dzogchen. This is how you should understand the view of Dzogchen. Dzogchen means "the great completion practice." Guru Padmasambhava taught that Dzogchen is the completion of the accumulation of both merit and wisdom. Loving-kindness and compassion are complete within Dzogchen. Otherwise, thinking that only the emptiness aspect is Dzogchen is not the Dzogchen view; it is nihilism. That would be *rdzogs chung*, "small completion," instead of *rdzogs chen*, "great completion."

All the great enlightened Dzogchen masters did the accumulation practices, such as the mandala offering and *ngöndro* practices. They adopted every aspect of the Buddha's teaching, and did not skip the preliminary practices by thinking that only the Dzogchen teachings are important. According to the great masters, that view is pointing toward nihilism. This is true not only because the great masters taught this, but also because your practice simply will not be successful that way. Realization will not arise if your view is partial, thinking that it is not necessary to accumulate merit. You might think you are in the Dzogchen state, but you are actually making your mind smaller than what the Dzogchen view is.

One of the Anuyoga tantras explains the result of practicing Dzogchen in the wrong way, through the story of Rudra Tarpa Nagpo. When Rudra Tarpa Nagpo first received the Dzogchen teaching, he became very excited about it. Then, because he considered that in Dzogchen there is nothing to do, no need to accumulate merit or perform generous activities, and no harm and no benefit, he misunderstood nonduality, the nature of everything being equal. He held the view of nihilism and began to engage in all sorts of negative activities. The result was that he became the demon Rudra.

Therefore, in the Nyingma lineage we practice all aspects of the Buddha's teaching and use these methods to bring realization of Dzogchen. A famous Nyingma master, Ngari Pandita Pema Wangyal, wrote a well-known book called *Definitive Distinctions among the Three Vows*. When explaining the title of the text, he said that one needs the vows of all three yanas to bring the ultimate realization of Dzogchen. The teachings of the three yanas are supporting methods to bring about the ultimate state of the Dzogchen view.

All the practices of accumulating merit and wisdom must conclude with primordial wisdom. In that way your practice is meaningful; you are practicing Dzogchen and touching the heart center of primordial wisdom. Your practice is complete, and that is the enlightenment of the Buddha.

ཨ་ཨ་ཨ༔

A A A

As a reminder to bring about the realization of primordial wisdom, the Vajrayana method uses the three syllables A A A. These invoke primordial wisdom, so that your entire visualization and meritorious practice are completed or transformed within the single nature of wisdom. The three A syllables symbolize the three doors of liberation or that all dharmas of the basis, path, and result are complete within great emptiness or the true nature.

After reciting the three A syllables, maintain that state for as long as you have time. Remain in that nature as it ebbs and flows without subtracting or adding anything.

Then, with vajra pride and vajra courage, again invoke Vajrakilaya using the same visualization as before. With that visualization and that attitude, you dedicate the merit, say the following prayers, and then do all your other activities for the sake of sentient beings.

Dedication and Aspiration Prayers

རྣམ་དཀར་དགེ་ཚོགས་རྒྱ་མཚོ་ཉིད༔

NAM KAR GE TSOG JA TSO NYI

I dedicate the vast accumulation of completely pure virtue

མཐའ་ཡས་སངས་རྒྱས་འཐོབ་ཕྱིར་བསྔོ༔

TA YE SANG JE TOB CHIR NGO

So that limitless sentient beings may attain enlightenment.

Whatever merit you gain by doing this practice is not kept for yourself alone, but you share that merit with all sentient beings for their enlightenment. This practice of dedicating the merit is a special teaching of Buddha Shakyamuni based on his limitless compassion and loving-kindness for others. A famous Indian master, Totsun Drubje, once praised the Buddha by saying, "I have read hundreds of books from different religious schools, but only you share the merit from your practice with all sentient beings. None of the other schools do this. You are the marvelously compassionate one; you are a friend to all sentient beings without their even knowing who you are." Guru Padmasambhava followed the same steps Buddha Shakyamuni taught, and also shared his merit with all sentient beings.

བདེ་དགེ་མཆོག་གསུམ་འདུས་པ་ཡིཿ

DE GE CHOG SUM DÜ PA YI

Embodiment of the happiness and goodness of the three jewels,

ཐུགས་རྗེའི་སྨོན་ལམ་དེང་འགྲུབ་ཤོགཿ

TUG JE MÖN LAM DENG DRUB SHOG

May your compassionate aspiration be fulfilled at this time.

The last two lines of the dedication are a special aspiration prayer: "By the power of this dedication, may every sentient being gain great joy and peace." The Tibetan words *de* and *ge* mean "happiness" and "goodness." According to Buddhist philosophy, happiness mainly applies to this lifetime, and goodness applies to the next lifetime or throughout many lifetimes. So, may there be happiness in this lifetime and both happiness and goodness throughout our lives until the attainment of enlightenment. May this aspiration be fulfilled by the power of the three jewels and their compassion.

Prayer of Auspiciousness

Before reciting the prayer of auspiciousness, once again say the interdependent co-origination mantra. This is done according to the tradition or pith instructions of the great lineage masters.

As always, you are saying auspicious prayers for all sentient beings in order to bring them happiness in this lifetime and in the future, here and everywhere. You perform this auspicious prayer with a clear understanding of primordial awareness-emptiness, and, therefore, it begins with the syllable HUNG.

ཧཱུྃཿ ཆོས་དབྱིངས་ཀློང་དགུའི་གཏེར་ཆེན་གྱིསཿ

HUNG CHÖ YING LONG GÜ TER CHEN JI

HUNG The great treasure of the nine spaces of dharmadhatu

ཟབ་རྒྱས་འགྲོ་ཀུན་སྨིན་མཛད་པ༔

ZAB JE DRO KÜN MIN DZE PA

Ripens all sentient beings by profound and vast activities.

དེང་འདིར་བཀྲ་ཤིས་བདེ་ལེགས་ཤོག༔

DENG DIR TA SHI DE LEG SHOG

At this time, may there be auspiciousness and happiness.

Chö ying is the "great dharmadhatu," and *long gü* refers to the "nine levels of true nature" as well as the "nine lineages." This discovered treasure contains nine lineages, which are none other than the true nature. Appearing on the relative level, the nine lineages have the aspect of the "nine spaces of dharmadhatu" or the "nine kinds of emptiness."

In the dharmadhatu itself, there are no divisions; the dharmadhatu is beyond categories. But according to students' capabilities for realizing the dharmadhatu, one can make divisions such as high, medium, and low capabilities. Each of those three can have three divisions, such as high high, medium high, low high, then high medium, medium medium, and so on. In this way, there are nine levels of space.

When you realize the true nature, you reveal the treasure of the dharmadhatu. Through revealing and practicing this teaching, may the profound and vast meaning mature all sentient beings and bring them happiness and auspiciousness everywhere.

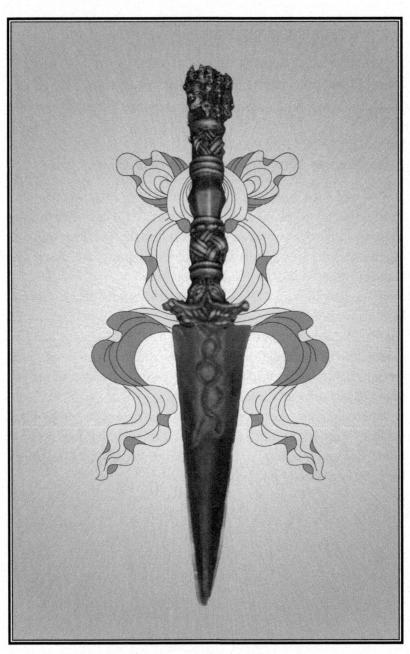

A phurba revealed by Tsasum Lingpa as terma,
one of the treasures of Gochen Monastery in Tibet

CHAPTER 4

The Four Phurbas

One approach to understanding the nature of Vajrakilaya is to understand the meaning of his name. In the Sanskrit language, he has two names: Vajrakilaya and Vajrakumara. Both names begin with *vajra* because the vajra corresponds exactly to the nature of Vajrakilaya—all the many meanings of *vajra* are contained in Vajrakilaya.

Vajra or *dorje* means "indestructible, very stable, and very condensed." The vajra has the power to destroy, but there is nothing that can destroy the vajra. *Kilaya* or *phurba* means "dagger" or "pointed." The phurba is very sharp, very pointed, and very powerful. Vajrakilaya means the indestructible phurba, the unshakable phurba, the phurba that is the embodiment of realization. Vajrakilaya's second Sanskrit name is Vajrakumara. *Kumara* or *zhönu* means "youthful." Realization of the vajra nature brings freedom from birth and death, so Vajrakumara is always youthful. Also, the vajra nature is youthful because it is indestructible. The Dzogchen teachings often refer to this nature as the youthful vase body.

The vajra is also known as "realization." In terms of realization, there are three Vajrakilaya states: the basic nature or basis of Vajrakilaya, the application or path of Vajrakilaya, and the fruition or result of Vajrakilaya. All three of these states have to be realized: the basis has to be realized, the path has to be realized, and that will bring the result, which is realization.

The realization of the basis, path, and result of Vajrakilaya can be discussed more specifically according to the four phurbas. The first phurba is the immeasurable compassion phurba, the second is the symbolic substantial phurba, the third is the bodhichitta phurba, and the fourth is the awareness wisdom phurba.

Each of the four phurbas contains all the qualities of the vajra, that is, they all have vajra nature, which is the essential nature to be realized. Vajra nature is not something that exists externally; realization of vajra nature is completely inherent, very stable, and condensed. All the buddhas of the ten directions, all the powers of the five buddha families, and both samsara and nirvana are condensed or embodied in these four phurbas.

THE IMMEASURABLE COMPASSION PHURBA

The first phurba is the *tsamed nyingje phurba*, the "immeasurable compassion phurba." The basic nature of all sentient beings is great purity. According to the Vajrakilaya lineage, this basic purity is known as *vidyottama*, "supreme awareness" (as in the tantra of the same name). Continuous supreme awareness is the basic nature of every sentient being. In that state, there are no distinctions between samsara and nirvana or between buddhas and sentient beings. Everything is continuous supreme awareness.

In accordance with that view, the Buddha gave the various Mahayana teachings of the second turning of the wheel of dharma, particularly the teachings of the *Prajnaparamita Sutra*.[55] He taught that everything is based upon great emptiness, and there are sixteen ways or twenty ways of understanding emptiness. These methods are used to achieve a clear understanding of the continuous nature of supreme awareness.

The Buddha broke down every possible notion—every kind of concept—such as high and low, dirty and clean, good and bad. He reduced them to the true nature in order to lead sentient beings from duality to nonduality. In the Prajnaparamita teachings, he gave about 108 different methods to attain realization of the basic kilaya nature.

Even though supreme awareness is the basic nature of reality, because we do not realize this, as sentient beings we develop dualistic thinking. We start making distinctions between subject and object, near and far, and so forth, and then we cling to those as real. The twelve links of interdependence arise, and, beginning with ignorance, we develop the notions of "me" and "mine," and all sorts of deluded thinking. The great master Chandra-kirti taught that you begin by clinging to the ego, then you cling to "what is mine," then to "what is other," such that there is an ongoing state of delusion. Due to clinging, our habitual patterns become stronger and stronger, and all our conceptions become regimented and solid.

In order to dispel ignorance and dualistic thinking, Vajrakilaya arises in a wrathful form. The wrath of Vajrakilaya is not the wrath of anger or jealousy; it is the wrath that destroys anger and jealousy. It is not like being angry with enemies and being attached to friends. This wrath is totally based upon great compassion. Directed toward duality, ego-clinging, grasping, and ignorance, Vajrakilaya's anger demolishes the causes of delusion throughout the six realms. Since it is based on immeasurable loving-kindness and immeasurable compassion, it is known as the phurba of immeasurable compassion.

To apply this phurba in a practical way, rather than becoming angry toward external situations, we begin by feeling great compassion for sentient beings. Then we start working with our own emotions to demolish ignorance, attachment, anger, jealousy, pride, fear, and doubts. We remove these emotions according to the way we interact with the world. At the same time, we expand our compassion for all beings in the six realms.

In order to cut the causes of delusion, we do not have to work directly with the six realms of sentient beings, but we need to work directly with our own minds. For example, when you become angry, do not pursue the anger. At that moment, look directly at the nature of the anger, and transform your anger into the continuous state of supreme awareness. By doing this, you actually remove the cause of the hell realms. This is a Dzogchen technique. Without denying the emotions, you can transmute them into continuous supreme awareness.

The emotions are none other than the mind. The nature of the mind is based on wisdom. The moment you understand this, you see that whatever appears is a display of wisdom, and in that moment whatever appears is liberated and transformed.

Since the emotions arise from wisdom, there is no reason to reject them or disparage them as bad. Instead, simply allow them to be transmuted within the natural state. The root text of the *Guhyagarbha Tantra*[56] states that from the beginning, in the primordially liberated state, there is nothing that is in bondage and nothing that is liberated. At the very moment when anger arises, we neither pursue nor hold on to the anger, but immediately transform it within its own nature. This is the Dzogchen technique of self-liberating one's emotions.

Otherwise, if we think that an emotion substantially exists on one side while its antidote substantially exists on the other side, and they are going to fight each other, then we are engaging in a very dualistic way of thinking. In Buddhism, this is known as the view of the Hinayana.

According to the Vajrayana view of the Dzogchen teachings, the moment a thought arises it is liberated in its own nature, without rejection or acceptance. For example, the nature of anger is really the continuous supreme awareness wisdom. That wisdom is Vajrakilaya—perfect, primordial, absolute Vajrakilaya—in which anger is completely destroyed. When anger is transmuted into mirrorlike wisdom, at that moment the hell realm completely disappears. Even the notion of the hell realm is completely absent from one's awareness.

By applying the same technique to attachment, the moment attachment arises it is transmuted into discriminating awareness wisdom, and the hungry ghost realm ceases to exist. When ignorance is transmuted within the continuous supreme awareness, dharmadhatu wisdom arises, and the animal realm disappears. In the same way, when pride is transformed into the wisdom of equanimity, the god realm disappears. When jealousy arises as the continuous supreme awareness—the absolute Vajrakilaya—then the *asura* or demi-god realm is destroyed, and jealousy becomes all-accomplishing wisdom.

With regard to the human realm, generally human beings have a lot of doubt, which is a mixture of wisdom and ignorance. Most of the time, doubt is an obstacle to your growth and makes realization difficult. Whenever doubts arise, if you transmute them into the supreme, absolute Vajrakilaya, then you have accomplished all five wisdoms. At that moment, the human realm no longer exists for you.

The phurba or kila has a very sharp point; it is very powerful and very accurate. When you use it to transmute your emotions into the primordial, absolute Vajrakilaya state, you immediately liberate all sentient beings into the wisdom of enlightenment. This aspect of Vajrakilaya practice is called the "phurba of infinite compassion."

THE SYMBOLIC SUBSTANTIAL PHURBA

The second phurba is the *tsenma dze kyi phurba*, the "symbolic substantial phurba." *Tsenma* can be translated as "symbol" or "characteristic." This means that all phenomena that appear have the characteristics of the phurba. Whether or not we recognize it, all things—mountains, trees, water, rivers, oneself—have the nature of the phurba. In essence, everything is in the pointed shape of the phurba.

For example, the human body is like a phurba. If you put your hands together and sit with your legs together, the lower part of your body is more pointed and the upper part is a little wider. Also, each of your fingers has the shape of the phurba. Other examples are the shapes of birds' beaks and claws. All beings, including animals, are within the phurba state.

The external world also has the nature of the phurba. When you look at trees, their overall shape points upward, and each leaf is pointed. In terms of the five elements, when water freezes into icicles in winter, it shows its pointed formation. Fire points upward as it burns. Although you cannot see wind, it feels sharp when it blows toward you. In the Abhidharma teachings, the shapes of the elements are discussed, and the wind is said to have the shape of a half-moon or a bow, which has points at each end. As for space, some Buddhist teachings say that space has the shape of a thousand spokes; but generally, space is divided by objects. When one looks at mountains, for example, the space around them looks pointed.

Phenomena naturally manifest in this way. Therefore, the *Kilaya Tantra* states that the entire universe is the symbolic substantial phurba.

Of course, there are also man-made phurbas, which did not develop naturally, but have been made to show the naturally existing phurbas more clearly. The created phurbas have a similar structure or shape, but they have different qualities, styles, and designs.

Some created phurbas have the head of Vajrakilaya, with either one face or three faces, at the top. The three faces on the top part of the phurba outwardly symbolize the three kayas. Inwardly, Vajrakilaya's three faces represent the three channels of the body. In terms of the practice or application, the three faces represent the ground, the path, and the result.

At the very top of the phurba is a half-vajra, which symbolizes the changeless nature of awareness wisdom. All aspects symbolized by the three faces are inseparable from the indestructible nature of awareness. The top of the phurba symbolizes the state of enlightenment.

Below the faces is a decahedron, a sphere with ten flat sides. It is like an octagon, but there are top and bottom sides as well. The ten sides symbolize the ten wrathful deities of Vajrakilaya; they are mentioned in the larger Vajrakilaya sadhanas. The decahedron as a whole represents the entire universe or the pure land where the buddhas reside. In the center of the decahedron is Vajrakilaya with his consort. Surrounding them are the five sons or princes of Vajrakilaya, the ten wrathful deities, the twenty-one mamos, and the sixteen dharmapalas. All of them reside within the decahedron, which is like a vast palace.

Some phurbas do not have the half-vajra and face, but simply have a small top, and then the decahedron. On both styles below the decahedron is a handle, decorated with lotus petals. The lotus is the symbol of love and compassion, actively manifesting as the buddhas and bodhisattvas. Below the handle is another decahedron, which symbolizes Vajrakilaya's retinue, as well as the dharmapalas. Below that, some phurbas have a crocodile mouth, but all phurbas end with three blades that meet in a point.

Generally, the phurba symbolizes that samsara and nirvana are united in one single nature. The top part of the phurba, from the half-vajra through the lower decahedron, represents nirvana or the pure land or wisdom. The part below the handle, beginning with the crocodile mouth, represents samsara. On the ultimate level, samsara and nirvana are not different. When one understands the nature of samsara, that understanding itself is nirvana. On the relative level, the compassion, loving-kindness, and wisdom of Vajrakilaya and realized beings are always with samsara. The crocodile mouth symbolizes the compassion of the bodhisattvas and realized beings; they never release themselves from samsara, and they never leave others behind. The crocodile mouth symbolizes compassion as the connecting point between nirvana and samsara.

The area below the handle symbolizes the three realms: the highest and most expansive is the realm of the formless gods, next is the realm of the gods of form, and lowest and smallest is the desire realm, which contains both gods and humans. The human area is smaller than the gods' area. The higher the realm, the more expansive it is. This also applies to the phurba state.

The way to transform the deluded state of samsara into the undeluded state of nirvana is symbolized by the three blades of the dagger. The three-sided dagger has many symbolic meanings. For instance, the nature of samsara is none other than the pure land of the three kayas. By understanding the supreme nature of Vajrakilaya, the three realms can be transmuted into the three kayas.

In terms of the view, the three blades symbolize the qualities of the three doors of liberation: not having characteristics, being beyond expectations, and having the nature of emptiness. This is the basic view of the continuous supreme awareness. The cause or basis has no characteristics, and the fruition or result is beyond expectations, so their identity or nature is emptiness. As they are without characteristics or expectations, cause and effect are both within emptiness. The entire universe is always based on great emptiness.

The three blades also symbolize the way to perform activities. When the phurba is used, it is always handled as an act of compassion. There are three types of compassion: compassion that focuses on sentient beings, compassion that focuses on the ignorance of sentient beings, and compassion with no focus or reference point—which can also be viewed as loving-kindness, compassion, and bodhichitta. Guru Padmasambhava taught that loving-kindness, compassion, and bodhichitta are the mind of the buddhas. Bodhichitta is free from delusion, but deluded beings like us can use bodhichitta to invoke supreme wisdom.

Every aspect of this symbolism is meant to show us that samsara and nirvana are one single state. There is not one part to reject and another part to accept. In the Mahayana sutras, Buddha Shakyamuni taught the importance of realizing the equality of samsara and nirvana. The Buddha Maitreya summarized this in the *Abhisamayalamkara* (*Ornament of Vivid Realization*)[57] by stating that samsara and nirvana are totally equal. And in terms of the pith instructions, the great master Saraha sang in one of his songs, "Samsara and nirvana are equal. That is Mahamudra, the great seal."

Whenever you see a symbolic substantial phurba, it is a reminder of your view, your meditation, and your realization, not just an interesting piece of sculpture.

In the tantras, the symbolic substantial phurba is commonly called the *tsenma dze kyi phurba*. But some tantras also refer to the substantial phurba as the *sipa phurba*. *Sipa* means "possible" or "existence." The sipa phurba is the phurba of all possible existence. It has also been translated as "cosmic phurba."

The phurba teachings are very vast, profound, and secret, and have many divisions. Although Vajrakilaya is wrathful, the existing phurba or sipa phurba can be used for different activities. There are four main types of activity: pacifying, increasing or enriching, magnetizing or overpowering, and subjugating. Sometimes phurbas are particularly dedicated to accomplishing the pacifying activity. These phurbas are usually white in color, and made of conch shell, crystal, or silver. Phurbas used specifically for increasing are yellow in color and made of metals such as gold. Red phurbas, which are used for magnetizing or overpowering, are made of copper or other red metals. Phurbas used for the purpose of subjugation are dark and made of a meteorite or iron, or very hard wood from thorny trees. Phurbas have various styles, materials, and purposes.

Substantial symbolic phurbas have specific measurements according to their different purposes. The measurements are based on the width of the fingers. They are two fingers long, four fingers long, six fingers long, and so on, up to sixteen fingers long. Each size has different purposes and different instructions.

Some substantial symbolic phurbas were discovered as terma objects. Most of these phurbas are made of meteorite, and when you look at the terma phurbas, you can see fabric imprints and fingerprints on them. History says that Guru Padmasambhava asked the dharmapala Dorje Legpa (Vajrasadhu in Sanskrit) to make these phurbas for him. Dorje Legpa was a famous blacksmith. Guru Padmasambhava wanted them to be made very quickly, so these phurbas are rather rough. When Dorje Legpa made them, he pounded them on his thigh. He was wearing a woolen chuba, and you can see the fabric patterns from his chuba on the phurbas. As soon as he finished the phurbas, he gave them to Guru Rinpoche, who would hold them and bless each of them. The fingerprints seen on these phurbas are those of Guru Padmasambhava.

The terma phurbas are very famous and very blessed. It is known that if you keep one on your body it will protect you from obstacles, even from bullets. This is not just a fairy tale. People experienced this when the Chinese Communists invaded Tibet, and this happened previously many times as well.

Meditation on oneself as Vajrakilaya is also the tsenma dze kyi phurba. All these aspects are included in the substantial symbolic phurba.

THE BODHICHITTA PHURBA

The third phurba is the *jangchub sems kyi phurba*, the "bodhichitta phurba," which has three aspects: outer, inner, and secret. In its outer aspect, the bodhichitta phurba is compassion—it is the intention to reach the state of the absolute Vajrakilaya for the sake of all sentient beings.

The inner bodhichitta phurba is the aspect of considering other sentient beings as being equal with you, and exchanging your own joy and happiness for their suffering. You give your happiness to others and take on their miserable or uncomfortable conditions yourself.

The secret bodhichitta phurba uses the vajra body to attain enlightenment. By understanding the inner structure of the body, the display of the different channels, the movement of the winds, and the all-pervasive nature of the essence element, and by applying the techniques as instructed, you can reveal the continuous supreme awareness. For example, by clearly knowing the essential nature and movement of the red and white elements, and how they are part of dualistic concepts, they can be united with the wind energy and dissolved in the central channel. The practice of the secret bodhichitta phurba is also known as *tummo* practice. Whether or not you use physical movements with that meditation, the dualistic concepts are transmuted in the central channel within the great bliss-emptiness. This is the secret bodhichitta phurba.

THE AWARENESS WISDOM PHURBA

The fourth type of phurba is the *rigpa yeshe phurba*, the "awareness wisdom phurba" or "continuous supreme-awareness kilaya." It is the final state. By practicing on the phurbas of compassion, substantial existence, and bodhichitta, the final goal is to actualize the absolute phurba state.

The awareness wisdom phurba is one's own primordial wisdom. This supreme awareness or primordial wisdom is all-pervasive and does not have any categories, distinctions, or regimentation. All those notions are transmuted into the pervasive nature of the mind of the buddhas. The famous Dzogchen master Shri Singha taught that the minds of sentient beings are broken into many pieces, but the Buddha's mind is all pervasive. Our minds are fragmented; when we look in one direction, we see some things, but not everything. When we listen, we hear some sounds, but not all of them. We do not have complete awareness wisdom.

The awareness wisdom phurba is beyond both grasping at existence and grasping at nonexistence. The renowned Dzogchen master Garab Dorje said that clinging to existent things is somewhat stupid, but clinging to nonexistent things is *really* stupid. In fact, he likened that to being even more stupid than a cow.

In the wisdom state, every aspect or dualistic notion is completely dissolved, like clouds that have disappeared into the sky. Once our notions and grasping have completely dissolved, then primordial, pristine cognition is revealed. That is the rigpa yeshe phurba.

PRACTICE OF THE FOUR PHURBAS

The word *phurba* can be translated as "dagger," a knife used to pierce something. In order to practice the four phurbas, a practitioner must know four things. First, you must understand the nature of each phurba. Then you must know the object to be pierced, and the signs indicating that the phurba has pierced its object. Fourth, if you are unable to accomplish this action, you should know the signs of failure or the errors to be corrected.

The awareness wisdom phurba has many synonyms, such as the true awareness phurba and Guru Padmasambhava's term, "the all-pervading wisdom phurba." Guru Padmasambhava said, "Now that you know what the phurba is, where will you put it?" The awareness wisdom phurba must pierce the dharmadhatu. This means that you must go beyond subject and object and realize the primordial nature, which is free of all complexity. The awareness wisdom phurba penetrates and merges with the dharmadhatu, which results in great equanimity.

The primary sign of accomplishment in relation to this phurba is transcendence of duality—the realization of the inseparability of the dharmadhatu and primordial wisdom. This is the first step to full realization of the dharmadhatu.

But if somehow you could not pierce the absolute dharmadhatu with the awareness wisdom phurba, why did that occur? Generally, the fault lies in clinging to dualistic concepts. Continuing to cherish thoughts of subject and object is a definite sign that you have not pierced the dharmadhatu deeply enough.

An important point to understand in relation to the Vajrakilaya teachings is that if you do not have the perfect view of the awareness wisdom phurba, you can practice for a long time without any auspicious signs arising. It may seem like the practice is boring and mundane. This happens if the way you invoke and understand rigpa is weak. To avoid this error, it is very important to have sufficient insight and understanding of the view before taking on the practice.

Next, the phurba of immeasurable compassion emanates from the state of the awareness wisdom phurba. Compassion is the inner power or play that arises from primordial wisdom. Guru Padmasambhava taught that the basis of the compassion phurba is original wisdom or enlightened mind, the same basis as that of the awareness wisdom phurba.

Where will you direct the immeasurable compassion phurba? The target of the immeasurable compassion phurba is all beings of the six realms. The six realms are caused by the six emotions, and as soon as we remove the emotional obscurations, our karma in these realms is liberated. Guru Padmasambhava explained that the sign of success in applying limitless compassion to the beings of the six realms is the spontaneous arising of unceasing love and compassion for all beings without any expectations or reluctance. This will not only be a subjective feeling, but externally you will perform beneficial activities according to the needs of beings. Free-flowing compassion is the sign of success in wielding this type of phurba.

If we are able to master the phurba of immeasurable compassion, we are qualified bodhisattvas. If you cannot immediately do all the loving things that you would like to do, but sincerely wish that you could help accomplish what is needed, then a good degree of loving-kindness and compassion is present. Upon full accomplishment, compassion arises unceasingly, like a great river flowing continuously.

A famous prayer from the Nyingma lineage, "The Prayer of the Butter Lamp," invokes the following: "May I become whatever will benefit all sentient beings. If it will benefit beings for me to be born as a king, may I become a king. If it is more beneficial for me to be born as a woman who becomes a queen, may it be so." It goes on to list rebirths of possible benefit to sentient beings—as a child, a lamp, medicine, a homeless beggar, or an animal such as a bird or a deer. "May I assume whatever forms are necessary to benefit beings." These wishes flow from great compassion. Even if your capacities are limited, you can still wish beings well and have positive visions regarding their future. Such thoughts are evidence of penetrating the six realms with the phurba of immeasurable compassion.

Having weak compassion, being reluctant to love, and having many expectations of others and little courage yourself are all signs that your practice with this phurba has not been successful. No matter how long you have been practicing and meditating, if you still have not learned to love and be compassionate, you are still a child and not yet strong in your practice.

The third phurba is the bodhichitta phurba. As we have discussed, bodhichitta may be understood as love, compassion, and wisdom. Bodhichitta is also connected with the all-ground, the *alaya* (Sanskrit) or *kunzhi* (Tibetan), which is the source or ground of all conditioned habitual patterns, as well as the source of all pure vision.

The all-ground that is the repository of habitual tendencies underlies our usual conceptions of everything, but through practice that source of habitual energy can be transformed into the open state of the pure ground of all. When that happens your emanations or displays will be based on pure perception or great perfection. The second form of kunzhi is also known in Tibetan as *kun gzhi byang chub sems*, which refers to the primordial wisdom represented by the awareness phurba. Jangchub sem (bodhichitta) is found in many Dzogchen texts to refer to the highest reality because bodhichitta is original awareness, the enlightened mind or buddha.

There is another meaning of bodhichitta, which is related to gaining a clear understanding of the vajra body, with its inner structure of channels, winds, and essence element (tsa, lung, and thigle). To practice the bodhichitta phurba we need to have a good understanding of the true nature of phenomena.

This understanding is that all phenomena are already within the mandala of Vajrakilaya. Both the external environment and the inner world of sentient beings are none other than Vajrakilaya. When you meditate on Vajrakilaya and Diptachakra, rather than mentally constructing them, you are actually discovering your original nature, which is always present and identical to Vajrakilaya and Diptachakra. Practice allows their transcendent qualities to come into focus so that you do not dilute the force of your understanding. Your recognition of the true nature can become one-pointed through the practice of visualization. Through visualization, the original structure or nature of all phenomena, sentient beings, and emptiness has a single focus, which is their mandala.

Another way to view the external world is as a blazing charnel ground —the pure land of Vajrakilaya—and to see all sentient beings as emanations of Vajrakilaya. The entire universe is always within the phurba state. This is also known as the "cosmic phurba" or the "external phurba," because it applies directly to the universe of sentient beings.

In particular, one's body is the vajra body or the vajra city where the enlightened ones reside. The shapes and forms of all things, including the human body, are based on the phurba structure. Our body is the city of Vajrakilaya and hundreds of millions of buddhas reside within it. The human body shares in the vastness of the pure land, and within it are infinite worlds of beauty. These manifest as the display of the purified channels, the blissful movement of the winds, and the unimpeded flow of wisdom energy. Throughout the galaxy of the pure land of the vajra body, the essence element or thigle radiates blessings and flashes lightning, which reveal the vajra nature of the body.

Diptachakra is the Sanskrit name of Vajrakilaya's consort. *Dipta* refers to a "mudra" or "seal" that marks everything, and here *chakra* means "wheel." Diptachakra represents that all things are marked by the true nature of dharmadhatu wisdom. The word *chakra* also implies "continuity" or "connection." Her nature does not just happen once or only occasionally, but the seal of dharmadhatu wisdom qualifies everything continuously. The entire universe remains united within that state.

Diptachakra's nature is also one of relationship and connection. The truth of this seal is inherent within us, and through practice we can transform all dualistic concepts and arrive at a clear understanding of the true nature—the awareness wisdom phurba or the mother of all the buddhas.

Just as there is a vast system of channels within our bodies, there are also many different chakras. For instance, there are five main chakras: the crown, speech, heart, navel, and secret chakras. The system of the five chakras is probably the one best known in Tibet. Some inner tantras, such as the *Kalachakra Tantra*,[58] mention a sixth chakra right above the head, which is known as the "chakra of space." Even ordinary sentient beings have a little light or energy operating in these higher centers;

however, when you reach enlightenment, all the chakras are transformed.

Buddha's *ushnisha*, the protuberance on the top of his head, is not made of flesh and blood, but represents the opening of the space chakra. It is also known as the "crown chakra of great bliss." The other chakras are the speech chakra of enjoyment, the heart center of the dharma, the navel chakra of emanation, and the secret chakra of great bliss. The crown chakra has thirty-two spokes, the speech center has sixteen spokes, the heart chakra has eight, the navel chakra has sixty-four, and the secret center has about sixty. The spokes are also described as petals.

The winds are the energy that travels through the channels. In Tibetan, the channels are called *tsa*. This has many profound meanings, but literally, tsa means "root"—the channels are the root of all the bodily systems. When you begin growing in your mother's womb, three channels form first: the navel channel and the channels of the two eyes. These become the principal channels going straight through the center of the body from the crown to the secret center. The chakras are located where the channels join, and appear in the form of wheels that link the parts of the vajra body. Each chakra is surrounded and interwoven with the three main channels, and there are many other channels that radiate from these three. There are 1,072 basic channels altogether.

The bodhichitta phurba is a vast and profound subject, which can be understood and practiced on many levels. One way is in terms of the two stages: the creation or visualization stage, and the completion stage. Visualization helps us understand that the entire universe, both internal and external, is the mandala of Vajrakilaya and Diptachakra. All visions and emanations arise from the great emptiness represented by Diptachakra.

The completion stage has two aspects: formless and with form. The completion-stage practice without form is the same practice as that of the awareness wisdom phurba.

The yogic practices involving the channels, winds, and essence element of the body are the completion-stage practices with form. Ideally, the creation stage is practiced simultaneously with the completion stage. When we understand ourselves to be the vajra nature or Vajrakilaya, we discover the channels, winds, and essence elements of the body, and this shows the union of the creation and completion stages of practice.

The phenomena displayed by the channels are principally due to the movement of the winds in the channels. Wind is a very important aspect of our body, mind, and life—without it there would be no movement or self-awareness. According to the Vajrayana, there are many kinds of winds. It has been calculated that a healthy person has about 21,600 breath cycles per day (inhaling, exhaling, and retention are counted as one cycle). Approximately every two hundred breaths, one subtle wisdom wind flows through, while the rest are considered karmic winds.

The winds are important because they determine our visions and the qualities of our experience. Our moods depend very much upon the condition of our winds. If you can recognize the wisdom wind that appears approximately every two hundred breaths and stay in that state, you have the opportunity to transform the emotional winds into wisdom wind.

Basically, there are three ways to practice the Vajrakilaya completion stage with an object. First we practice completion stage with the channels, then in relation to the winds, and finally with the essence element of the body.

Practice on the essence element of the body is tummo, the yoga of psychic heat. *Tummo* is a Tibetan word that literally means "cruel lady." This is associated with wrathful deities whose function is to burn away all dualistic concepts. The deity is cruel by not letting us dwell in the world of duality, not letting us stay where we like to hang out.

The essence element pervades the body, but in practice it is primarily located in the crown chakra, in the form of the Tibetan syllable HAM written upside down. Four finger widths below the navel center is the seat of tummo, whose nature is heat and bliss. It resides there in the shape of the Tibetan short AH and produces a fire that travels up the central channel to the crown chakra. When the fire reaches the syllable HAM and unites with it, the white essence element melts and drips through the body. As it descends, it gives rise to the realization of emptiness united with great bliss.

This process happens in terms of four or sixteen levels of great bliss.

These are caused by the movement of the winds through the main channels, circulating through the different junctures, descending and ascending, and generating various forms of bliss-emptiness.

Once you become familiar with the true nature of the channels, winds, and essence element and stabilize your understanding of great emptiness, there are instructions concerning how to contact a qualified consort with whom to practice. These practices also involve the invocation of Vajrakilaya, although it is not required that you meditate on the channels, syllables, and so forth. The instructions for practice with a consort involve the visualization of oneself and one's consort in the form of Vajrakilaya and Diptachakra and abiding in that meditation. This is another form of practicing on the bodhichitta phurba.

The ultimate result of practicing on the channels is to understand the channel system as a matrix of wisdom. The result of the wind-energy practice is the actualization of clarity or luminosity in the wisdom channel. The result of the essence-element practice is to merge with the dharmakaya.

Perfect mastery of the bodhichitta phurba is demonstrated by being able to pierce the space of Diptachakra, which means to realize Mahamudra. This is the understanding that the entire universe arises within bliss-emptiness. This is the nature of the union of Vajrakilaya and Diptachakra. The ability to manifest the entire mandala of Vajrakilaya and his retinue is a sign of accomplishing the bodhichitta phurba.

From the union of Vajrakilaya and his consort, ten wrathful deities with consorts emanate in the ten directions, as well as the four sons and four gatekeepers. From there, ten emanations with fangs and ten emanations with wings arise, which are known as predators and scavengers. Reemanating from that part of the mandala are the sixteen dharmapalas of Vajrakilaya. Piercing the space of Diptachakra with the bodhichitta phurba spontaneously generates this retinue of wrathful deities who are all emanations of the bodhichitta phurba. If somehow we are unable to accomplish this, we have not pierced the dharmadhatu with the bodhichitta phurba. This is quite simple and easy to understand. If you can do it, you will; if you cannot, you won't.

The symbolic substantial phurba can be understood in many different ways. Phurbas are fashioned according to the specific activities for which they will be used, such as pacifying, increasing, overpowering, and subjugating. The substance from which the phurba is made endows the implement with different qualities. Phurbas made of wood can have various associations, as there are peaceful woods, semiwrathful woods, and wrathful woods. Each substantial phurba must be made in perfect proportions and designed in a way that corresponds with the obstacle to be overcome.

The basic object to be overcome by the substantial phurba is the negativity rooted in ego-clinging. Ego-clinging appears in many ways, and these may be understood as the demonic forces, whether visible or invisible, that cause problems for sentient beings and disrupt their joy and peace. Negativity and obstacles are called the objects of liberation.

In the Vajrayana, different symbols or clay sculptures of the objects to be liberated, called *lingas* in Sanskrit, are used. They are fashioned in the form of human beings or animals and put in a special kind of triangular iron box. The practitioner does the self-visualization of Vajrakilaya and consort in their mandala, and with the three powers of meditation, mantra, and substance, the practitioner summons the negative forces and the obstructing energies to be dissolved into the linga.

To practice the symbolic substantial phurba, one must first practice the other three phurbas: the awareness wisdom phurba, the immeasurable compassion phurba, and the bodhichitta phurba. All these phurbas must be accomplished first. These three are considered the upper part of the Vajrakilaya practice, which is the actualization of enlightenment. The lower part of Vajrakilaya practice involves subjugating demons. Without achieving the upper part, one should not attempt to perform the lower part.

Trying to accomplish this subjugation practice without accomplishing the other three phurbas turns the making of lingas into a child's game, like building sand castles on the beach. To meaningfully engage in such a practice, the practitioner has to abide in the enlightened nature and engage in these activities in a very powerful and vigorous manner. In doing so, one embodies the nature of Vajrakilaya completely, not just in one's imagination.

NYAG JNANAKUMARA

This is a story about the great master Nyag Jnanakumara, who was one of Guru Padmasambhava's twenty-five original disciples, as well as one of his nine heart students. This is the same Nyag who is mentioned in the Nyingma lineage prayers. Nyag Jnanakumara was the disciple who was able to draw nectar from solid rock, but as this story shows, even highly realized beings may have karmic residues to purify.

At the time this story took place, in the early part of the ninth century, Guru Padmasambhava had left Tibet. Nyag had become a renowned Buddhist scholar and was living in a hermitage near his native village. Before Nyag had become Guru Padmasambhava's student, many ministers and officials regularly visited him, but that changed. His family was opposed to the Buddhist teachings and favored the traditional Bön religion. One day, a group of Nyag's relatives suddenly came inside his meditation hut and turned everything upside down. When they found a small skull cup containing some red liquid they said, "Look at this! He is killing human beings and using the blood! How savage!" They made up stories and completely destroyed the hermitage. They acted as if they were going to kill him, so he ran away.

Nyag arrived in southeastern Tibet, and was joined by an attendant who was also his student. As they traveled together through the upper part of Chimyül in Kongpo, they wandered into an empty valley and came upon seven female goats. Nyag said to his student, "Bring those goats over here. We do not have anything to eat, and we can drink their milk."

The student said, "Master, I don't think we should take these animals. Maybe somebody owns them." Nyag replied, "I really don't think so. Who would put seven goats in this empty valley? There is no one out here. I think we should grab them." So they took the goats and used their milk.

After a few days, the owner, a man named Chim Jarog, came searching for his goats. He saw the two men who had been keeping his goats near their cave. He thought, "So these are the rascals who stole my goats!" and he was terribly angry. He destroyed their hermitage and came after Nyag with an iron hammer, so Nyag had to take off running again.

Nearby was a hunter who was about to shoot a large deer, but when Nyag and his disciple ran by, they scared the deer away. The hunter was enraged and wanted to kill Nyag, but Nyag kept running. This was all very upsetting. He had been chased out of retreat, the goatherd tried to beat him to death, and the hunter also threatened his life. Feeling very sad, Nyag went to southern Tibet to meditate and practice.

At that time, Mune Tsenpo, the eldest son of King Trisong Deutsen, was the king of Tibet. According to history, Mune Tsenpo ruled only eighteen months before his mother poisoned him because of his progressive ideas. Many people came to the royal funeral ceremony. The great master Vimalamitra had already left for China, but because the king had died, he was invited back to perform the funeral rites. When Nyag heard that Vimalamitra had returned to Tibet, he immediately went to see his teacher. Nyag and Vimalamitra had worked together on the translations of many texts. During that process, Nyag had received numerous teachings from Vimalamitra. So, Nyag journeyed to central Tibet to see his master.

Upon arriving, he did prostrations and sat down. Vimalamitra was well aware of what Nyag had been through, but he pretended he didn't know anything. He just said, "How are you doing?" Nyag replied, "I am well, but I have not been having a very good time. I've had obstacles." When Vimalamitra asked what had happened, Nyag told him everything.

Finally, Vimalamitra said, "I am sorry to hear that these things have been happening to you. You are a true master with great knowledge as well as a fine translator. Such obstacles may not hurt you personally, but they have a negative effect on the establishment of the buddhadharma. You need to show some strength and signs to the people who are doing these things to you."

Nyag asked, "Please give me some instructions on how to do that." And Vimalamitra said, "You need to practice on Vajrakilaya. I will instruct you."

So Nyag, his attendant, and Vimalamitra went to a cave at Kharchu in Lhodrak and practiced the mandala of the twenty-one phurbas. Vimalamitra gave them teachings, and the three of them practiced together for three weeks. On the twenty-first day, they actualized the Vajrakilaya state and saw the entire retinue of Vajrakilaya's emanations. The phurbas on the shrine began knocking together, and the entire mandala of wrathful deities appeared dancing before them.

Now, to have truly achieved the phurba state you must know how to wield the phurba. In order to test the truth of his student's understanding, Vimalamitra told Nyag, "Wield the phurba to see if you have realized it in action or not." Nyag was still a little upset about the incident with the seven goats. The name of the man who owned the goats translates as "the Crow of Chim." This was the first thing that came to Nyag's mind, so he brandished his phurba and cried out, "This is for the Crow!" Suddenly many crows gathered in the sky before them. Nyag pointed the phurba at one particular bird, rotated it and said, "This is for the Crow of Chim!" And immediately the bird dropped to the ground and died. When Vimalamitra saw this, he said, "You can obviously kill, but now you must bring that bird back to life." But Nyag was unable to do that. Vimalamitra said, "Without the ability to bring creatures back to life, you shouldn't use the phurba in this way. To do so is no different than the action of a murderer." Then Vimalamitra picked up a small amount of dust and threw it toward the crow, which got up and flew into the sky.

Vimalamitra gave Nyag more detailed instructions on how to practice Vajrakilaya, and Nyag applied himself to his meditation until he reached the ultimate state of Dzogchen, where all phenomena dissolve into primordial awareness. He also achieved the rainbow body.

Nyag was already a great master, but perhaps as a demonstration to others, he had troubles that led him to reshape his practice. His example shows that when using the symbolic substantial phurba to pierce negativities and obstacles, one must have this same kind of ability.

Nyag Jnanakumara became a renowned master of the phurba, and his lineage spread throughout Tibet. Many recent tertöns have brought forth Nyag's phurba lineage teachings. In particular, His Holiness Dilgo Khyentse Rinpoche discovered and taught phurba teachings from the Nyag-Phur lineage, which descends directly from Nyag Jnanakumara.

ACTIVITIES OF THE SYMBOLIC SUBSTANTIAL PHURBA

In order to do the practice of the symbolic substantial phurba correctly, it is important to have actualized the upper part of the Vajrakilaya practice. Then, if we have the ability, we can perform extraordinary activities if there is a good reason to do so. Otherwise, we do not even think of using the symbolic substantial phurba in a destructive fashion, but understand it symbolically.

The symbolic substantial phurba can destroy visible and invisible beings, negativities, and demons. But it is also part of these practices to remove difficulties and bring balance. For example, when you actualize the power of Vajrakilaya, you can master the elements, stop natural disasters, and remove mental and physical sickness.

The sign of successfully piercing with the symbolic substantial phurba is to do as you wish in relation to the elements. For example, you can point the phurba and stop fire from burning, stop water from flowing, or stop the spread of disease. These are signs of mastering the symbolic substantial phurba.

The power of the symbolic substantial phurba was abused in Tibet. Some misguided practitioners sought to conquer rivals and gain power through using the symbolic substantial phurba. To be involved in such thoughts and activities only strengthens ego-clinging and one's own suffering. This is the exact opposite of the realizations associated with the awareness wisdom phurba, the immeasurable compassion phurba, and the bodhichitta phurba.

If you abuse the phurba in this way, rather than accomplishing what you desire, it will bring the three bad results known as "being blocked," "returning," and "scattering." While being blocked is bad, to have the energy return to you is worse, and the very worst is when the energy is scattered or spread out.

"Being blocked" means that anything you try to practice is ineffective; you are weak and timid and stuck in a blank state. Your phurba practice is not sharp enough to pierce the object.

"Returning" means that the energy you use to overcome someone or further your own reputation does not achieve that end, but comes back and destroys you instead. Vajrakilaya represents love, compassion, and wisdom; using this power for personal gain only intensifies ego-clinging and suffering, which is the opposite of Vajrakilaya.

"Scattering" or "spreading" means that ego-clinging hurts not only you, but it hurts your friends, your family, your neighbors, and your country. The harm spreads throughout your environment and various aspects of your life.

To avoid these faults, you must practice the awareness wisdom phurba and the limitless compassion phurba in union. If you understand both of them perfectly, then you can engage in the bodhichitta phurba. When you are accomplished in the bodhichitta phurba, you can begin to practice the lower part of Vajrakilaya, which is concerned with subjugating negativity and demonic forces. When you have mastered the awareness wisdom phurba, the immeasurable compassion phurba, and the bodhichitta phurba, the activities performed with the symbolic substantial phurba will be powerful and go smoothly, benefiting beings now and in the future. This is the result of authentic practice.

RECEIVING THE EMPOWERMENTS OF THE SYMBOLIC SUBSTANTIAL PHURBA

When you practice Vajrakilaya, it is good to have at least two symbolic substantial phurbas—one to remain on your shrine and one to carry with you. The phurba on the shrine may be used once in a while when receiving the empowerments at the end of the practice session, but at other times, you should not use or touch it. Consider it to be Vajrakilaya himself.

Receiving the empowerments is usually done once a week instead of every day, or on certain days such as the new moon and the eighth, ninth, tenth, fifteenth, nineteenth, or twenty-fifth days of the lunar month. Hold the phurba with two hands and always keep the point down. Visualize each of your arms as a Tibetan letter AH and join them together. This symbolizes the union of the male and female buddhas, Samantabhadra and Samantabhadri. You can also visualize a moon disc in your right palm and a sun disc in your left so that the phurba is embraced by the sun and moon, which are also symbols for the buddhas Samantabhadra and Samantabhadri.

In a more detailed visualization, the fingers of the right hand consist of male deities in the form of the five dhyani buddhas—the index finger is Vairochana, the middle finger is Ratnasambhava, the ring finger is Amoghasiddhi, the small finger is Amitabha, and the thumb is Vajrasattva—while the fingers of the left hand are their female wisdom consorts. By uniting them all together, we invoke Vajrakilaya, because Vajrakilaya embodies them all.

Toward the end of the sadhana, there is a special prayer to chant while receiving the empowerments. Hold up the phurba while visualizing Vajrakilaya as the embodiment of Samantabhadra and Samantabhadri and the ten male and female dhyani buddhas. Then bring the phurba down to bless the three centers at your forehead, throat, and heart.

You can also raise the phurba to your crown chakra and rotate it clockwise three times. As you do this, visualize thick rays of wisdom light radiating in all directions, recollecting the blessings of the buddhas. You can repeat this triple rotation at your forehead, on the right and left sides of your body, and at your waist. This removes attachment to appearances and clinging to emptiness, and merges appearance and emptiness in one state of great equanimity and primordial union.

There are different meditations associated with rotating the phurba. The right side is connected with male negativities and Buddhists, the left side with female negativities and non-Buddhists, and the waist is associated with the pairs of male and female, Buddhist and non-Buddhist. Turning three times to the right protects oneself and turning three times left protects others. Three times at the waist protects everyone within the nature of Vajrakilaya.

While receiving the empowerments, when you visualize the phurba radiating light, understand it to be Vajrakilaya, who embodies all ten dhyani buddhas as well as Samantabhadra and Samantabhadri. He is the union of skillful means and wisdom, the living buddha emanating wisdom light that steadily grows more powerful and glorious. When you recite the mantra, move the phurba to your forehead as you say KAYA (body), to your throat as you say WAKA (speech), and to your heart center as you say TSITTA (mind). With SIDDHI HUNG touch all three places again to confirm the blessings of body, speech, and mind.

After that, respectfully put the phurba back on the shrine exactly where it should be. It is important not to let anyone other than yourself touch this phurba. Even other sangha members should not touch it. Keep it as a special object on your personal shrine.

Wisdom Dakini Yeshe Tsogyal

CHAPTER 5

Vajrakilaya Practice

OBSTACLES AND SIGNS

When you begin to practice Vajrakilaya and learn to unite the awareness wisdom phurba and the limitless compassion phurba, the signs of accomplishment are not always beautiful, even if you have received clear teachings from qualified masters, and your practice is good. There are many different signs that arise, some of which may be very pleasant, while others may be very uncomfortable. Therefore, do not expect anything in particular. Continue to uphold your commitment with courage, refresh your awareness, and carry on without hopes or fears. If you begin to wish for good signs and are discouraged by bad signs, then you are caught in aversion and attachment.

In his Dzogchen teachings, Guru Padmasambhava urged his disciples to keep going beyond the boulders on the road of meditation. In Tibet, there are lots of boulders on the roads, but in America, we would probably say "the potholes in the streets." Experiencing these difficulties is a sign that you are actually moving. Whether the road is smooth or bumpy, it is good that you are moving along. When you begin the practice of Vajrakilaya these obstacles will manifest. At such times, maintain your strength and renew your commitment. You need stability and continuity to overcome these episodes.

There are many ways in which signs can occur. Difficult situations can arise externally, internally, and secretly. Externally, things may happen that you did not expect, or things may not proceed the way you want them to. You may find that when one problem is solved, another problem arises. On the inner level, you might have health problems, discomfort, insomnia, long and involved dreams, and other unusual phenomena. The secret signs show up in the emotions. You may have more expectations and anxiety about the teachings. You may have doubts about the teacher and other sangha members, less certainty about what you are doing, or less compassion than before. These signs do not mean that you are losing the ability to love and be kind. When we come to these rough places in the road, we should always persevere, strengthen our practice, and keep moving toward our goal.

Positive signs of achievement may also occur. Externally, there may be periods where everything goes along nicely. Inwardly, your body feels peaceful and healthy, and it functions well. Emotionally, you feel relaxed, and anger, jealousy, and other emotions do not disturb you as they did before. We should not cling to positive signs, but maintain the ultimate view in every situation from now until we attain enlightenment.

The strongest and most positive signs of achievement are the three signs known as the body, speech, and mind signs of Vajrakilaya. Among the signs of the body are that the practitioner's physical form becomes very bright, light, joyful, and peaceful. One has visions, dreams, or direct perceptions of the emanations of Vajrakilaya. Also, one's phurba on the shrine might spark and radiate light. These phenomena were quite common in Tibet. Almost every monastery had special phurbas that danced on the shrine. These are all signs of the physical achievement of Vajrakilaya.

The signs of the speech achievement of Vajrakilaya involve the practitioner's speech becoming very powerful and perfect, and one's expressions of wisdom spontaneously expanding. For example, there are yogis who can write beautiful dharma songs that send special messages to sentient beings. Hearing the Vajrakilaya mantras, such as the syllable HUNG, resounding from the shrine or from trees, mountains, or open space is another sign that one has achieved the speech of Vajrakilaya.

The initial signs of achieving the mind of Vajrakilaya are temporary experiences of joy, peace, and a very relaxed state of mind. The ultimate sign of accomplishing the mind of Vajrakilaya is a perfect understanding of the nonduality of the awareness wisdom phurba and the immeasurable compassion phurba. Boundless compassion arises for all beings while the mind abides in the expanse of wisdom beyond concepts. The moment anything arises, it is liberated in the very space of its appearance. At the same time, unceasing great compassion arises for all beings without any expectation or reluctance.

There are also special signs, such as a pure understanding that the teacher, the teachings, and the sangha are all part of the mandala of Vajrakilaya. Another is the ability to perform the four actions of Vajrakilaya: pacifying, increasing, overpowering, and subjugating. You become efficient at whatever you do.

These are signs of having achieved a measure of the realization of Vajrakilaya. In any case, it is important not to become overinvolved with the appearance of signs, whether good or bad, but simply continue to practice and meditate.

VAJRAKILAYA AND THE FOUR DEMONS

When you first see a wrathful deity, you might wonder why it is wrathful. The purpose of wrathful deities is to directly remove obstructions and negative influences. They quickly transform all phenomena into the padma family aspect of discriminating wisdom, so that delusion has no chance to arise. To accomplish this great transmutation, the deities appear wrathful and highly energetic.

Obstacles arise in four basic ways, which are known as the four demons: clinging to one's aggregates, clinging to one's emotions, the fear of death, and being distracted. These demons are none other than our own neurotic projections. So we invoke Vajrakilaya to uproot our neurotic mind and destroy ego-clinging. This is the purpose of the four phurbas associated with Vajrakilaya.

The four demons or *düzhi* exist due to the obscurations of the mind, but through practice they can be instantly transformed into the primordial nature of Vajrakilaya. His wrathful power immediately purifies the external effects of neurosis. If you have a strong visualization practice and cultivate deep levels of meditation, then you can smash the four demons internally as well.

This is similar to a situation where an enemy is attacking you. If you are prepared, you can challenge his attack and seriously weaken his stance. Similarly, if you cultivate an understanding of the primordial nature and continually invoke this insight, you will recognize the projections as they arise. By knowing their strength and their source, the demonic forces will be unable to move you. You will be able to weaken and eventually transform the four demons.

When Buddha Shakyamuni became enlightened under the *bodhi* tree, on the outer level he subdued all the demonic forces through the power of loving-kindness, while on the secret level he invoked the absolute nature of Vajrakilaya and annihilated them on the spot.

When Guru Padmasambhava practiced Vajrakilaya in Nepal, it is said that he encountered three demonic forces that were represented by the sky, the earth, and the space in-between. Through the practice and actualization of the state of Vajrakilaya, Guru Padmasambhava subdued these three powerful demons externally, internally, and secretly. Outwardly they are called the three demonic forces, inwardly they are known as the three demons, and secretly they are the three poisons. Experiences such as nightmares, bad omens, emotional problems, sickness, and discomfort are all attributable to demonic forces. All of these, whether internal or external, are manifestations of one or more of the demonic energies.

In the visualization, these demonic forces are represented by the gyaltsen, the two corpses under Vajrakilaya's feet, as described in the line-by-line commentary. The gyalpo is the male aspect and the tsenmo is the female aspect.

The gyalpo represents anger, arrogance, and a touch of jealousy. Jealousy is the opposite of love and compassion; it arises when you see that someone is successful, and you wish they would not be so happy. Such emotions are represented by the gyalpo, which is Tibetan for "king" (perhaps this is because kings are typically arrogant and want to be the best and most important of all).

The tsenmo represents grasping, attachment, and discontent, and arises when you feel that something is always missing, and things are never good enough, and then you grasp all the more tightly. This mental attitude is represented by the tsenmo demon.

In short, these two demons represent attachment and anger, and ignorance is the common basis of both. Without ignorance, these two would never arise. Visualizing these energies in human form does not mean that every man or woman is a demon, but that everyone is influenced by emotions such as attachment and anger which are based in ignorance. The demons lying under Vajrakilaya's feet signify that Vajrakilaya is inherently free from attachment, anger, and ignorance. If we can work with the energy of attachment and anger, we will be able to undermine and transform ignorance. This is another reason why Vajrakilaya is a very important and powerful practice.

Guru Padmasambhava predicted that during the degenerate era to come, the gyalpo and tsenmo aspects would grow more powerful and cause more obstacles. Anger would be more common and violent, attachments would get stronger, and all kinds of misfortunes would descend on the beings and the world.

What is the degenerate era? This does not refer to objectively existing, external time. It is not time which is degenerating, but the overall mentality of human beings. This trend is internal and is reflected externally in our experience of the world.

Vajrakilaya practice deals directly with these different obstacles. It is not a gradual practice for working on transforming the emotions; instead, it directly removes our obstacles. Anger and attachment must be instantly cut the moment they appear. In Dzogchen this is known as *trekchö* or "cutting thoroughly." This is instantaneous; cutting thoroughly does not take any time.

When emotions arise, do not give them a chance to develop. To do this, Guru Padmasambhava taught that you have to act directly and immediately. Do not give the emotions an opportunity to linger. If you think, "I'll see this clearly later," you are already under the control of the emotions. If you wait and reflect, you allow the passions to develop, and eventually they will rule you. Instead, as soon as emotions arise, invoke your understanding of the true nature, apply the trekchö technique, and be liberated in that instant. Do not trace the emotion's development or give the impulse to follow it time to grow, but instantly liberate the energy of the emotion into its original condition.

To practice the creation-stage visualization of Vajrakilaya properly, we need to destroy our clinging to attachment and anger. At the present time, we believe that anger and attachment are real and that they solidly exist. This belief in the true existence of our mental states is what we have to destroy. There are no dark, demonic forces that exist like suspicious-looking aliens. Liberation happens when we stop clinging to our emotions as being real.

The way to practice Vajrakilaya is to recognize his fundamental state at the same moment that you visualize him, which means that we have to deal with emotions and neuroses instantly. This is not a gradual approach, but an immediate action of recollecting the true nature of Vajrakilaya, which cuts through anything that may arise. Vajrakilaya practice combines the techniques of Mahayoga, Anuyoga, and Atiyoga. It employs the Dzogchen technique of instantly invoking the primordial nature, which simultaneously liberates one from the dualistic concepts that obscure the recognition of that nature. These obstructions are simply the primordial nature unrecognized by us. By recollecting the nature of Vajrakilaya, we instantly transform all conditions and liberate them directly into their original state.

Vajrakilaya has one face, two arms and two legs. He is in coemergent union with his consort, Diptachakra, who also has one face, two arms, and two legs. This form, though relatively rare, is not exclusive to Tsasum Lingpa's terma revelations. Many other great tertöns have revealed the two-armed, two-legged form. As mentioned earlier, in the sadhana associated with the well-known Vajrakilaya tantra, the *Twelve Kilayas Tantra*, Vajrakilaya has this same form. Vajrakilaya and Diptachakra in union symbolize the immeasurable compassion phurba and the awareness wisdom phurba united together. This is important to remember from the beginning to the end of your visualization practice. Wisdom and compassion are merged in one state of awareness wisdom, which is identical with the ultimate primordial nature. This union is described as coemergent or "born together."

The nature of Vajrakilaya is the dharmakaya—it is free of all complexities. This is the right view and inner meaning of Vajrakilaya and the awareness wisdom phurba. It does not involve describing solid objects or physically existent entities. The forms and names associated with Vajrakilaya point to the ultimate realization of the true nature, the awareness wisdom phurba—enlightenment. Even if you have not achieved full realization and only have a momentary experience of the primordial awareness wisdom phurba, during that moment all negative emotions are instantly destroyed. This is why the Vajrakilaya teachings state that the moment you recollect the awareness wisdom phurba, vajra wrath will totally cut anger and destroy attachment. No matter how strong or tough they seem, they are completely wiped out, just as the sun drives away all darkness.

PRACTICING ACCORDING TO THE
NATURE OF VAJRAKILAYA

Vajrakilaya is the embodiment of the three jewels—buddha, dharma, and sangha—as well as the three roots of guru, yidam, and dakini. When you practice Vajrakilaya, you are practicing all of these; none of them are excluded. When you begin the Vajrakilaya sadhana, it is important to understand this so that you will naturally be incorporating all the other practices.

We practice Vajrakilaya on both the relative and absolute levels. On the relative level, we begin by developing bodhichitta, the spirit of loving-kindness and compassion. Bodhichitta practice is not simply good preparation for Vajrakilaya; Vajrakilaya *is* bodhichitta. We cannot sidestep bodhichitta. One excellent means of cultivating bodhichitta is through tonglen, the practicing of exchanging, or sending and receiving.

To cultivate bodhichitta, start by seeing all beings as equal to yourself, then work on seeing them as more important than yourself. By gradually developing this attitude toward everyone, you will eventually understand the phurba of immeasurable compassion. This is extremely important. Do not feel that practicing bodhichitta is separate from practicing Vajrakilaya or that it is only a preliminary practice. Compassion is the essence of Vajrakilaya practice.

From the absolute point of view, Vajrakilaya is the ultimate truth of primordial awareness. The whole cosmic display—the entire universe—appears within the great bindu of emptiness from which everything spontaneously manifests. Without seeing the primordial purity of the mind and all phenomena, we cannot realize the state of Vajrakilaya. Every aspect of the phurba of immeasurable compassion emanates from this pure, nondual wisdom. When we abide in that state we awaken great unceasing compassion for all sentient beings. This is the practice of the absolute Vajrakilaya.

When the wisdom dakini Yeshe Tsogyal asked Guru Padmasambhava to explain the nature of Vajrakilaya, Guru Rinpoche replied, "The absolute state of dharmakaya, free from all complexity, is the very nature of Vajrakumara." Guru Padmasambhava was echoing a famous tantra, the *Vidya Uttama[maha] Tantra (Tantra of Primordial Awareness)*,[59] which is a tantra that describes Vajrakilaya as the absolute state of the original nature—the indestructible, indivisible dharmadhatu. From that state, immense and wrathful energy blazes forth. This tells us exactly how we should imagine the form as well as the activity of Vajrakilaya.

The dharmadhatu or dharmakaya of Vajrakilaya is one of the four phurbas, the rigpa yeshe or awareness wisdom phurba. Vajrakilaya embodies the two truths: the immeasurable compassion phurba is the relative truth, and the awareness wisdom phurba is the absolute truth. These two truths encompass every aspect of phenomena in samsara and nirvana.

Vajrakilaya practice merges the relative and absolute levels of meaning. In the creation-stage practice, the union of relative and absolute is visualized in the splendid form of Vajrakilaya and his consort. Visualizing deities with heads, arms, and legs is a skillful way of symbolizing the union of relative truth and absolute truth. The male and female deities together in union are Vajrakilaya. It is not that the male deity alone is Vajrakumara and the female is not, or the other way around. Both are the same nature, manifesting in two different ways in order to clarify the understanding of the practitioner.

The wrathfulness of Vajrakilaya is known as "vajra wrath" because it destroys deluded anger and jealousy. Many of the Vajrakilaya tantras state that "Vajra wrath cuts aggression." The vajra wrath subdues ordinary anger in such a way that it leaves no trace. It cuts deep down to the very root of anger.

For example, at the moment when anger arises, if we do not pursue it but look back to the source of the anger itself, then the anger is transformed into luminous emptiness. This is also known as the awareness wisdom phurba. If we have this kind of realization, the awareness wisdom phurba is no different than Madhyamaka, Mahamudra, or Dzogchen.

To put this into practice, it is important not to separate Vajrakilaya from this world. The entire world or samsara is the palace or mandala of Vajrakilaya. Nirvana is also none other than this world. Samsara and nirvana exist equally within the nature of Vajrakilaya.

For instance, to think that "I am going to practice Vajrakilaya and go beyond samsara," may be fine for the time being, but it is not the perfect view according to the nature of this practice. Since the entire universe is the palace or the pure land of Vajrakilaya, there is no other place to go. The entire universe has the form, shape, and color of Vajrakilaya; Vajrakilaya pervades the entire world.

The way to recognize that the world has the nature of Vajrakilaya is through awareness. Awareness is the absolute state of Vajrakilaya. The awareness wisdom phurba is primordially within our being. In order to reveal our primordial awareness, we do the visualization practice according to the instructions given in the Vajrakilaya tantras.

To do this, it is necessary first to understand the nature of one's own mind. The nature of one's mind is the source of all the emanations of Vajrakilaya. When meditating, one needs to see that Vajrakilaya is inseparable from one's own perceptions, one's own mind, and one's awareness. These are united in the one true nature, without any separations, and everything is transformed into the state of Vajrakilaya.

While we meditate on ourselves as Vajrakilaya, at the same time we invoke the blessings of the Buddha Vajrakilaya and all the buddhas. We invoke them to mix inseparably with us, like water being poured into water.

When we invoke the power of Vajrakilaya, maintaining ourselves in the primordial nature, there is nothing to be afraid of and nothing to be attached to. All the mental states of human beings can be summarized into two aspects: hope and fear. Hope is based on attachment, and fear is based on anger and feeling threatened. Hope and fear are major obstacles to our enlightenment. Even in the ordinary world, they hinder our good results.

Vajrakilaya is a very powerful practice for removing hope and fear. Vajrakilaya practice leads to the vast state of openness where hope and fear do not exist. Within the primordial nature, everything is included in the mandala of Vajrakilaya. Everything is complete and liberated in that state. By practicing Vajrakilaya, we are liberating our awareness, even in a worldly way, from hope and fear. This powerful practice naturally pacifies all obstacles, in the same way that the brightness of the sun naturally clears away darkness. This is the real nature of Vajrakilaya.

Once we go beyond hope and fear, we are within the state of great bliss. Hope and fear are like nets that have trapped our nature within samsara. When hope and fear are removed, all kinds of expectations and emotional states naturally dissolve; in other words, we reach nirvana. Nirvana is nothing other than liberating our awareness from the nets of hope and fear and emotions.

Right now we are in the realm of dualistic thinking. In order to go beyond concepts, we have to begin our practice by using the concepts of loving-kindness and compassion. Although love and compassion are concepts, they can skillfully lead us to the nonconceptual state.

We have to expand our thoughts of loving-kindness and compassion to include all sentient beings. In order to fulfill these compassionate thoughts and activities, we practice according to the nature of Vajrakilaya. Loving-kindness and compassion are the nature of Vajrakilaya. They radiate the energy of the primordial Vajrakilaya, so that our practice focuses on the light of Vajrakilaya, or what is called "the dawn of Vajrakilaya." As soon as we begin practicing loving-kindness and compassion for all sentient beings, the absolute state of Vajrakilaya begins to dawn.

The best and most essential way to practice Vajrakilaya is to clearly understand the nature of Vajrakilaya and to base your practice on non-clinging and love and compassion.

Phurba from the shrine of Phurba La Khang
Medicine Buddha Temple at Padma Samye Ling

CHAPTER 6

A Story of the Phurba Yogi

In terms of showing the activity aspect of the buddhas, it is sometimes said that the yogis of Vajrakilaya are more powerful than the yogis of Yamantaka, the wrathful form of Manjushri. Vajrakilaya represents the activity aspect of all the buddhas, and Yamantaka Heruka represents the body aspect of all the buddhas. On the absolute level, there is no distinction between them. However, there is a story about the differences between two practitioners, one of Vajrakilaya and one of Yamantaka.

About nine or ten generations after Guru Padmasambhava left Tibet, there lived a famous master named Langlab Jangchub Dorje, who was called "the phurba yogi." At the time of this story, he had already reached a high realization of Vajrakilaya practice, but from the ordinary point of view he was just a regular layperson. He worked as a shepherd and was rather poor.

During this same time, there was a famous master named Ra Lotsawa Dorje Drak,[60] who had reached high realization through the practice of Yamantaka. However, when he was unhappy, he would signal his displeasure through signs of his realization. He was extremely moody (for example, some say that it was Ra Lotsawa's power that precipitated the death of Marpa's son).

Ra Lotsawa was invited to the village where Langlab lived. One afternoon, Ra Lotsawa was giving teachings to a large crowd; he was seated on a high throne and surrounded by his retinue of many students. Everybody was being very respectful to him, except Langlab, who arrived toward the end of the teaching. Langlab did not offer any prostrations or show any respect. He just stood and listened for a little while and then started to leave.

When Ra Lotsawa saw this he started to feel slightly moody. He asked people who Langlab was, thinking that maybe Langlab was very stupid and did not realize what a great teacher he, Ra Lotsawa, was. But people replied that Langlab was not stupid—he was a practitioner and just a regular person.

Upon hearing this, Ra Lotsawa thought Langlab was being arrogant, so he decided to show some signs of his realization in order to deflate Langlab's arrogance. He started to do an uncommon kind of fire-offering practice (called *yagja* in Sanskrit), but he could not make it work successfully. He tried a second time, but could not accomplish it. On his third attempt, when he still could not show any signs to Langlab, suddenly Vajrakilaya descended from the sky above Ra Lotsawa, appearing with the lower part of his body in the form of a phurba blazing with wisdom fire as in the HUNG practice. From the point of the phurba, drops of lava began to fall on Ra Lotsawa, who became frightened and told Langlab, "I apologize and take refuge in you."

Thus it was recounted how the master of Vajrakilaya triumphed over the power of the master of Yamantaka. People also said that after this experience Ra Lotsawa stopped being so moody.

CHAPTER 7

Questions and Answers

Student: Can you speak about the channels, winds, and essence element of the body?

Khenpos: The channels, winds, and essence element—or tsa, lung, and thigle—are all based on the primordial wisdom of great emptiness. The winds are always in motion, but this movement is more subtle than ordinary, outer motion. It is the source of the display of wisdom as enlightened activity. The essence element is the source of great bliss, which is beyond the ordinary sensations of bliss. The ultimate state of the essence element is the great bliss-emptiness of primordial wisdom. It is not subject to change, so we cannot say it is permanent or impermanent. This is why it is called "the great permanence." The siddha king Indrabhuti said, "Great bliss is not impermanent," which implies that it is permanent. But this permanence goes beyond relative permanence and impermanence. The higher teachings use the Sanskrit prefix *maha* or the Tibetan suffix *chenpo*, which means "great," to symbolize what is beyond duality.

Going beyond relative characteristics is emphasized in all the Buddha's teachings, not only the Vajrayana. In the *Prajnaparamita Sutra*, Buddha told one of his disciples, "Oh! Subhuti, if you perceive forms as being permanent or impermanent, you are still attached to characteristics." In the *Uttaratantra Shastra* (the *Sublime Continuum*), the future buddha Maitreya taught that buddha nature is the great purity beyond clean and unclean, the great bliss beyond happiness and suffering, the great permanence beyond permanence and impermanence, and the true identity beyond identity and nonidentity. All of these statements point beyond duality.

The nature of the channels, winds, and essence element is great emptiness, and practice must proceed based on this understanding in order to be effective. The great masters have emphasized that we must transcend the sense consciousnesses. To do these practices it is necessary to have some understanding of primordial awareness, or rigpa. The displays of the channels, winds, and essence element are the play of rigpa itself. With that understanding, the practitioner can go beyond sensations.

Student: **If you are aware of the wisdom wind as it comes through every two hundred cycles, does it bring a state of equanimity?**
Khenpos: Yes, if you are able to recognize that state, you can experience stability instantly.

Student: **Is it possible in practice to reduce the two hundred karmic-wind cycles so that the wisdom wind arises more frequently?**
Khenpos: Yes, there are many teachings on how to work with the wind system, such as the "big vase" (*bum chen*) and "small vase" (*bum chung*) practices, which are designed to increase the wisdom wind and reduce the emotional winds. The emotional karmic winds are very powerful. For that reason, Nagarjuna, Guru Padmasambhava, Saraha, and the great siddhas taught that the root of samsara lies in the winds. Instability in the winds creates our hallucinations and visions. You can observe this in your own meditation practice. If your thoughts are very active, you can breathe through your mouth instead of your nose. This can calm the whirlwind of neurotic thoughts.

Student: **In terms of the four activities, why are "magnetizing" and "overpowering" considered to be the same activity?**
Khenpos: Basically, this refers to the activity of inspiring others toward the dharma. This means that others gravitate toward you, so it can be called "attracting" or "magnetizing," but basically, it is an activity of overpowering. The Tibetan word is *wang,* which means "power."

The Buddha taught that what you are trying to overpower is your own mind. In Vajrakilaya practice, "overpower" should not be taken too literally—you are not supposed to go out and crush something. This actually means overpowering your own ego-clinging and your own perceptions.

At the present time, you cannot overpower your own mind; it is too scattered, it is running all the time. Even when you feel that you are controlling your mind somewhat, it is sneaking out the back door and running off somewhere else. If you can overpower your own mind, then you will have much greater ability. For example, when you die you will have more control over your journey in the bardo and your rebirth. However, most of us do not have that capability right now. We need to magnetize or overpower our scattered minds.

Student: **Would you clarify the difference between magnetizing and subjugating?**
Khenpos: Magnetizing or overpowering is gentler than subjugating. You are controlling your mind, yet allowing things to stay as they are a little bit longer while watching carefully. Subjugating means that something is transformed into something totally different, such as the five emotions being transformed into the five wisdoms. Their identity is changed. With magnetizing, your intention is to eventually transmute them, but you are not going to do so immediately. You use the emotions as part of your practice and then transmute them.

Student: **When would we use the bell and damaru in this practice?**
Khenpos: Mostly during the visualization of the deities. In particular, when you are visualizing yourself as the deity and invoking the blessings, and when saying the Sanskrit mantras related to the visualization, you use the bell and damaru.

Student: **How do you bridge the dualistic thought that Vajrakilaya is separate from yourself?**
Khenpos: In the first place, there is no reason to think that you are separate from Vajrakilaya. There is no doubt as to whether or not you are

Vajrakilaya. You are pure primordial wisdom, or rigpa—you *are* Vajrakilaya. The primordial nature of your mind is the nature of Vajrakilaya. As soon as you invoke your primordial wisdom, at that moment your dualistic concepts, grasping, and ignorance are dispelled. There is no place for ignorance and dualistic thinking to stay in the face of primordial wisdom. It is like the sun—as soon as it arises, the darkness is gone.

That is the way our primordial wisdom is in reality, but on the relative level we believe that we have obstacles and obscurations, so we invoke Vajrakilaya. We need to practice Vajrakilaya on the relative level because that is how we change our mental patterns. However, as soon as we invoke Vajrakilaya, in that moment everything is naturally and spontaneously completed.

Student: When I visualize Vajrakilaya, there is a sense that he does exist in front of me, radiating his wisdom and blessings. Is that true as well?
Khenpos: Yes, you need to have the sense that Vajrakilaya is there, performing all these powerful activities, radiating wisdom, and subduing demons. You do need to think that. At first, your meditation is more related with your imagination. To go in the right direction, you have to start by imagining that Vajrakilaya is there. However, all practice is based upon the state of great emptiness—primordial wisdom, which is your basic nature. As you practice more, you will be radiating more and more of your inner wisdom. Finally, your imagination and your inner wisdom will merge into one single state, and you will reach the real Vajrakilaya state, or enlightenment.

Student: How does the Buddha's teaching of cause and result fit in? Do cause and effect happen only on the relative level?
Khenpos: Yes, cause and effect are relative truth. Absolute truth is beyond cause and effect. However, in order to bring the realization of absolute truth, you have to understand relative truth. Where we are now—our starting point—is relative truth. A clear understanding of relative truth is part of the cause, which will bring realization of the absolute as its effect.

Student: When you start to understand cause and result, and see how they create samsara and nirvana, do you begin to align yourself with bodhichitta?
Khenpos: Yes. It is important to understand how causes and conditions work on the relative level, both externally and internally. Throughout your practice, you actualize bodhichitta as both the cause and condition of bringing about the effect of enlightenment.

Student: Rinpoches, what are the signs of accomplishment from doing this practice?
Khenpos: There are many signs. For instance, you will have various dreams. The various signs depend upon the way an individual practices, upon his or her dedication, devotion, and concentration. For example, if someone meditates very well on Vajrakilaya's body, when he or she looks at a thangka of Vajrakilaya, the deity will be dancing and emitting lightning and flames. This happened many times in Tibet; when great masters would meditate, the phurbas on their shrines would move, dance, and make loud, laughing noises. In the great monasteries, the monks would have a group meditation on Vajrakilaya. The sangha members would join together and practice day and night, without stopping, for twenty-one days. Toward the end of the practice session, the mantra would be self-reciting from the phurbas on the shrine mandala. The monks could hear the mantra resounding without anybody reciting it, without any tape recorders or anything like that. Sometimes they would hear only the HUNG syllable, and sometimes the entire Vajrakilaya mantra. This is a sign of achievement of the speech aspect of Vajrakilaya.

When signs of accomplishment occur, they will benefit you individually by pacifying your obscurations, your illnesses, and all of your obstacles. They will increase your life, fortune, and realization. You will be able to magnetize or overpower your own phenomena and your own mental and emotional states, and subdue your ego-clinging and the negative forces of dualistic concepts. These benefits are not only for you personally, but through your realization you will be able to benefit your family, your neighbors, your groups, your cities, and your countries.

The sign of receiving the mind blessings of Vajrakilaya is that your love and compassion—your bodhichitta—gradually or even instantly increase for all sentient beings. Another sign is that you have more pure perception and less grasping and clinging. Suddenly, you have very good realization; your meditation becomes powerful, stable, and comfortable, and joy and peace arise. These are signs that you are receiving the blessings of the mind of Vajrakilaya.

Dedication and Aspiration Prayers

All existing phenomena arise as the mudra of the blazing Heruka.
Unceasing sounds and echoes are transformed into the music of Kilaya.
Recognition of one's own awareness is the absolute wisdom Kilaya.
May everyone actualize this state, having spontaneously accomplished all the
*   buddha activities.*

May the secret treasures of all the victorious ones,
Their incomparably supreme teachings,
Arise as the sun in the sky,
Gloriously pervading the entire universe.

By this merit, may all attain omniscience,
May it defeat the enemy, wrongdoing.
From the stormy waves of birth, old age, sickness, and death,
From the ocean of samsara, may we free all beings.

Vajrakilaya Sadhanas

ক্লু་མེད་ཡང་ཕུར་གྱུའ་དམར་ནག་ལས༔

From The Dark Red Amulet
of Unsurpassable Yang-Phur

རོ་རྗེ་དཔའ་བོ་ལྷན་ཅིག་སྐྱེས་སྦྱོར་བཞུགས༔

THE COEMERGENT UNION OF
THE VAJRA HERO

ཨོ་རྒྱན་རྩ་གསུམ་གྱིང་པ་ཆོས་ཀྱི་རྒྱ་མཚོས་གཏེར་མའོ།།

Orgyen Tsasum Lingpa Chökyi Gyatso

By practicing on this may all sentient beings
achieve the perfect true-nature state of the lama.
May their highest aspiration be fulfilled
for the benefit of all sentient beings.

༄༅། །ཚིག་བདུན་གསོལ་འདེབས་བཞུགས་སོ།

TSIG DÜN SÖL DEB ZHUG SO
Seven-Line Prayer

ཧཱུྃ༔ ཨོ་རྒྱན་ཡུལ་གྱི་ནུབ་བྱང་མཚམས༔

HUNG   OR JEN YÜL JI NUB JANG TSAM
HUNG   On the northwest border of the country of Udiyana,

པདྨ་གེ་སར་སྡོང་པོ་ལ༔

PEMA GE SAR DONG PO LA
On the pistil of a lotus,

ཡ་མཚན་མཆོག་གི་དངོས་གྲུབ་བརྙེས༔

YA TSEN CHOG GI NGÖ DRUB NYE
You have attained the most marvelous, supreme siddhis.

པདྨ་འབྱུང་གནས་ཞེས་སུ་གྲགས༔

PEMA JUNG NE ZHE SU DRAG
You are renowned as the Lotus Born,

འཁོར་དུ་མཁའ་འགྲོ་མང་པོས་བསྐོར༔

KHOR DU KHA DRO MANG PÖ KOR
Surrounded by your retinue of many dakinis.

ཁྱེད་ཀྱི་རྗེས་སུ་བདག་བསྒྲུབ་ཀྱིས༔

CHE CHI JE SU DAG DRUB CHI
Following you in my practice,

ཕྲིན་གྱིས་རློབས་ཕྱིར་གཤེགས་སུ་གསོལ༔

JIN JI LOB CHIR SHEG SU SÖL
I pray you will come to confer your blessings.

གུ་རུ་པདྨ་སིདྡྷི་ཧཱུྃ༔

GU RU PEMA SIDDHI HUNG

PRAYER TO THE LAMAS OF THE LINEAGE

ཀུན་བཟང་རྡོར་སེམས་དགའ་རབ་ཤྲཱི་སིང་།

KÜN ZANG DOR SEM GA RAB SHI RI SING
Samantabhadra, Vajrasattva, Pramodavajra, Shri Singha,

པདྨ་ཀ་ར་རྗེ་འབངས་ཉི་ཤུ་ལྔ།

PEMA KA RA JE BANG NYI SHU NGA
Padmakara, the Twenty-five, King and subjects,

སོ་ཟུར་གནུབ་གཉགས་གཏེར་སྟོན་བརྒྱ་རྩ་སོགས།

SO ZUR NUB NYAG TER TÖN JA TSA SOG
So, Zur, Nub, Nyag and the hundred tertöns and others,

བཀའ་གཏེར་བླ་མ་རྣམས་ལ་གསོལ་བ་འདེབས།

KA TER LA MA NAM LA SÖL WA DEB
The lamas of Kama and Terma (lineages), to you I pray

PRAYER TO TSASUM LINGPA

རིགས་བརྒྱའི་ཁྱབ་བདག་ཨོ་རྒྱན་ཆོས་ཀྱི་རྗེ།

RIG JE CHAB DAG OR JEN CHÖ CHI JE
Inseparable from Orgyen Padmasambhava, supreme lord of the hundreds of buddha families,

གཏན་གྱི་སྐྱབས་མཆོག་རྩ་གསུམ་གླིང་པ་ལ།

TEN JI CHAB CHOG TSA SUM LING PA LA
To you, Tsasum Lingpa, the supreme object of refuge,

གསོལ་བ་འདེབས་སོ་འཆི་མེད་རིག་འཛིན་སྩོལ།

SÖL WA DEB SO CHI ME RIG DZIN TSÖL
I pray to grant me the immortal blessings of the vidyadhara state,

རྟག་ཏུ་འབྲལ་བ་མེད་པར་བྱིན་གྱིས་རློབས།

TAG TU DRAL WA ME PAR JIN JI LOB
So that I may remain inseparable from you.

དཔལ་ཆེན་རྡོ་རྗེ་གཞོན་ནུའི་དགོངས་པ་ཡིས༔

PAL CHEN DOR JE ZHÖN NÜ GONG PA YI
From the profound state of realization of splendid Vajrakumara,

ལྷུན་གྲུབ་ཕྱག་རྒྱ་ཆེན་པོའི་རིག་འཛིན་དང༔

LHÜN DRUB CHAG JA CHEN PÖ RIG DZIN DANG
From the spontaneously accomplished and mahamudra vidyadharas,

རྡོ་རྗེ་ཐོད་ཕྲེང་རྩལ་ལ་བྱིན་བརླབས་ཏེ༔

DOR JE TÖ TRENG TSAL LA JIN LAB TE
The lineage blessings are passed to the Vajra Skull Garland Mighty One (Dorje Tötreng Tsal).

འདས་དང་མ་འོང་ད་ལྟ་དུས་གསུམ་གྱི༔

DE DANG MA ONG DA TA DÜ SUM JI
To all the past, present, and future, the three times

ཕྲིན་ལས་བརྒྱུད་པའི་བླ་མ་ལ་གསོལ་བ་འདེབས༔

TRIN LE JÜ PE LA MA LA SÖL WA DEB
Lamas of the activity lineage, I pray.

ཨོ་རྒྱན་པདྨ་འབྱུང་གནས་ལ་གསོལ་བ་འདེབས༔

OR JEN PEMA JUNG NE LA SÖL WA DEB
To Udiyana Padmakara I pray.

PRAYERS TO THE ROOT LAMA

འོག་མིན་ཆོས་ཀྱི་དབྱིངས་ཀྱི་ཕོ་བྲང་ན།

OG MIN CHÖ CHI YING CHI PO DRANG NA
In the palace of the Ogmin dharmadhatu,

དུས་གསུམ་སངས་རྒྱས་ཀུན་གྱི་ངོ་བོ་ཉིད།

DÜ SUM SANG JE KÜN JI NGO WO NYI
The essence of all the buddhas of the three times,

རང་སེམས་ཆོས་སྐུ་མངོན་སུམ་སྟོན་མཛད་པའི།

RANG SEM CHÖ KU NGÖN SUM TÖN DZE PE
The one who shows clearly the dharmakaya of my own mind,

རྩ་བའི་བླ་མ་ཞབས་ལ་གསོལ་བ་འདེབས།

TSA WA LA MA ZHAB LA SÖL WA DEB
We pray to the honorable root guru.

དཔལ་ལྡན་རྩ་བའི་བླ་མ་རིན་པོ་ཆེ།

PAL DEN TSA WE LA MA RIN PO CHE
Glorious root teacher, precious one,

བདག་གི་སྤྱི་བོར་པདྨའི་གདན་བཞུགས་ལ།

DAG GI CHI WOR PEME DEN ZHUG LA
Dwelling on the lotus seat on the crown of my head,

བཀའ་དྲིན་ཆེན་པོའི་སྒོ་ནས་རྗེས་བཟུང་སྟེ།

KA DRIN CHEN PÖ GO NE JE ZUNG TE
Hold me with your great kindness.

སྐུ་གསུང་ཐུགས་ཀྱི་དངོས་གྲུབ་རྩལ་དུ་གསོལ།

KU SUNG TUG CHI NGÖ DRUB TSAL DU SOL
Bestow the accomplishments of body, speech, and mind.

ཀླུ་མེད་ཡང་ཕུར་གུ་ལུ་དམར་ནག་ལས༔

From The Dark Red Amulet
of Unsurpassable Yang-Phur

རོ་རྗེ་དཔའ་བོ་ལྷན་ཅིག་སྐྱེས་སྦྱོར་བཤུགས༔

THE COEMERGENT UNION OF
THE VAJRA HERO

ཨོཾ༔ སྭཱཧཱ་ཀྲཱི་སཱུ་ཧྲཱི༔ ཀླུ་མ་བཙོམ་ལྷན་འདས་རྫོ་རྗེ་གཞོན་ནུའི་ལྷ་

ཚོགས་ལ་ཕྱག་འཚལ་ལོ༔   ས་མ་ཡ༔

I prostrate to the Guru Bhagavat, Dorje Zhönu, and the hosts of deities.
SAMAYA སམཡ༔ ༀ༔ ༔

བདག་འདྲ་ཨོ་རྒྱ་གར་མཁས་པ་ཡིས༔ཡང་སྙིང་དཔའ་བོ་ལྷན་ཅིག

སྐྱེས་སྦྱོར་གྱི༔ བསྒྲུབ་པའི་ཟབ་རྒྱ་གནད་ཀྱི་མན་ངག་བསྟན༔ དབྱངས་

ཅན་མཚོ་རྒྱལ་མི་བརྗེད་གཟུངས་ཀྱིས་ཟུངས༔ ཡི་གེར་ཐོབ་ལ་རིན་

ཆེན་གཏེར་དུ་སྦོས༔ ལས་ཅན་ཐུགས་ཀྱི་སྲས་དང་འཕྲད་པར་ཤོག༔

I am a learned one from India.
From the inner essence, the hero of coemergent union,
I will teach the pith oral instructions of this profound and vast secret practice.
Sarasvati, Yeshe Tsogyal, retain this with your unforgetting wisdom.
Write it down and conceal it as a precious terma.
May a karmically connected heart son find this.

དང་པོ་བསྙེན་པའི་བཅའ་གཞི་ལག་ལེན་ནི༔ ཉམས་དགའ་དབེན་པའི་
གནས་སུ་བག་ཕབ་སྟེ༔ འབྲུ་ཚོམ་ཁ་རུ་བུམ་གདན་དཀྱིལ་འཁོར་བཤམ༔
དེ་སྟེང་རྣམ་རྒྱལ་བུམ་པ་རྫས་ཀྱིས་བཀང༔ ཁ་རྒྱན་མགུལ་ཆིངས་ལ་
སོགས་གཞུང་བཞིན་བཀྲམས༔ ཚོགས་དང་མཆོད་རྫས་སྨན་གཟིགས་
གང་འཛོམས་བཀྲམ༔ བགེགས་བསྐྲད་བྱ་ཞིང་སྲུང་འཁོར་བསྐོམས་
ནས་སུ༔ མཆོད་རྫས་དམིགས་པའི་བྱིན་བརླབས་དལ་དུ་འཇུག༔
ས་མ་ཡ༔

First are the customary preparations, the foundation of the practice.
Relax joyfully in a solitary place. Arrange the mandala of the vase
platform on heaps of grain, and on top of that, place the victorious vase
filled with substances and adorned with mouth ornaments, neck
ribbons, and so forth, as described in the text. Gather and arrange the
feast offering, offering substances, and beautiful objects—whatever you
have. Expel the obstructing spirits and visualize the protection circle.
Having mentally blessed the offering substances, enter the mandala.
SAMAYA

ক্সুব্ষ্ণ্দ্র্র্র্ণ্ঃ

Refuge

ན་མོ༔ གདོད་ནས་ལྷུན་གྲུབ་གཉུག་མའི་རྩ་བ་གསུམ༔

NAMO DÖ NE LHÜN DRUB NYUG ME TSA WA SUM

NAMO The primordial, self-existing, innate three roots

ཀུན་ཏུ་རང་སེམས་མ་གཡོས་སྐྱབས་སུ་མཆི༔

KÜN TU RANG SEM MA YÖ CHAB SU CHI

Are always, without wavering, one's own mind. Thus, I take refuge.

སེམས་བསྐྱེད་ནི༔

Bodhichitta

ཧོ༔ འཁོར་འདས་མཉམ་ཡང་ཕྱོགས་ལྷུང་བྱེ་བྲག་གནད༔

HO KHOR DE NYAM YANG CHOG LHUNG JE DRAG NE

HO Samsara and nirvana are the same; one's perspective is the main difference.

ལེགས་པར་རྟོགས་པས་དེ་བཞིན་སེམས་བསྐྱེད་དོ༔

LEG PAR TOG PE DE ZHIN SEM CHE DO

Realizing this fully, I arouse bodhichitta.

[Dispelling the Obstructing Spirits]

ཧཱུྃཿ   ང་ཉིད་ཡེ་ནས་རྡོ་རྗེ་གཞོན་ནུའི་སྐུཿ

HUNG   NGA NYI YE NE DOR JE ZHÖN NÜ KU

HUNG   Primordially, I am Dorje Zhönu,

ཐུགས་རྗེའི་རང་རྩལ་འགྱེད་པ་པོ་ནའི་ཚོགསཿ

TUG JE RANG TSAL JE PA PO NYE TSOG

Emanating hosts of compassionate energy,

བར་མེད་ཁྱབ་པས་བགེགས་ཚོགས་མ་ལུས་ཀུནཿ

BAR ME CHAB PE GEG TSOG MA LÜ KÜN

Who pervade everywhere and summon all obstructing spirits

ཨ་འཐས་གཞོམ་ཕྱིར་གཏོར་མ་ལེན་པར་ཁུགཿ

A TE ZHOM CHIR TOR MA LEN PAR KHUG

To receive this torma, in order to destroy ego-clinging.

ཨོཾ་བཛྲ་ཏ་ཀི་རཱ་ཛ་ཧཱུྃ་ཛཿ

OM VAJRA TAKI RADZA HUNG DZA

གཉིས་འཛིན་རུདྲ་ཨཱ་ཀར་ཥ་ཡ་ཛཿ

NYI DZIN RUDRA AH KARSHA YA DZA

ཧཱུྃ

HUNG   NYING JE JIN YÜL MA RIG GEG CHI TSOG
HUNG   Hosts of deluded obstructing spirits, objects of
             compassionate generosity,

TOG ME DE ZHIN TOR ME TSIM PAR DENG
Be satisfied with this torma of nonconceptual suchness, and leave.

CHI TE MI DRO ZHEN PE CHING SI NA
If, fettered by attachment, you refuse to go,

RIG PA DOR JE TSÖN CHAR DE ZHOM SHIG
You will be destroyed by the weapon of vajra awareness.

OM VAJRA WIDHO JNANA KUMARA SARVA BIGHNEN
TSINDHA TSINDHA HUNG PHET

[Setting the Protection Boundary]

ཧཱུྃ༔ རྡོ་རྗེ་གསུམ་གྱི་དཀྱིལ་འཁོར་བདག༔

HUNG   DOR JE SUM JI CHIL KHOR DAG

HUNG   The lord of the mandala of the three vajras

ཡེ་ནས་མ་བཅོས་གཞལ་ཡས་ཁང༔

YE NE MA CHÖ ZHAL YE KHANG

Resides in the primordially unfabricated palace.

རང་བཞིན་རླུང་ལྔས་སྲུང་བའི་གུར༔

RANG ZHIN LUNG NGE SUNG WE GUR

With the protection tent of the nature of the five winds,

སོ་འཐབ་འཁྲིགས་པས་མཚམས་ཆོད་ཅིག༔

SO TAB TRIG PE TSAM CHÖ CHIG

Densely intermeshed, close the boundary.

ༀ་བཛྲ་ཏྲ་ཡ་མཎྜལ་ཡོཾ་པ་ཙུ་སཏྭ་བཛྲ་རཀྵ་ཡེ་སྭཱ་ཧཱུྃ༔

OM VAJRA TRAYA MANDALA YAM PENYETSA SARVA VAJRA RAKSHAYE SWAHA

[Blessing the Offerings]

།རྃ་ཡྃ་ཁྃ༔

RAM YAM KHAM

ལན་གསུམ༔

Three times

ཨོྃ་ཨཱཿ་ཧཱུྃ༔

OM AH HUNG

ལན་གསུམ་གྱིས་སྦྱང་༔

Three times to purify

ཨོྃ་མ་ཧཱ་ཀ་ལཀྵ་བཉྫེཙ་ཨ་མྲྀ་ཊ་ཨཱཿ་ཧཱུྃ༔

OM MAHA KALAKSHA PENYETSA AMRITA AH HUNG

ཨོྃ་བཛྲ་པུཥྤེ་དྷུ་པེ་ཨ་ལོ་ཀེ་གནྡྷེ་ནཻ་ཝི་ད་ཤབྡ་ཨཱཿ་ཧཱུྃ༔

OM VAJRA PUSHPE DHUPE ALOKE GANDHE NAIVIDYA
SHABDA AH HUNG

ཨོྃ་སརྦ་བཉྫེ་མྲྀ་ཊ་ཧཱུྃ་ཧྲཱི་ཐཿ

OM SARVA PENYETSA AMRITA HUNG HRI THA

ཨོྃ་མ་ཧཱ་རཀྟ་ཛྭ་ལ་མཎྜ་ལ་ཧཱུྃ་ཧྲཱི་ཐཿ

OM MAHA RAKTA DZOLA MANDALA HUNG HRI THA

ཨོྃ་མ་ཧཱ་བྷ་ལི་ཏ་ཏེ་ཛྭ་བྷ་ལི་ཏ་བྷ་ལ་བྷ་ཏེ་གུ་ཧྱ་ས་མ་ཡ་ཧཱུྃ་ཧྲཱི་ཐཿ

OM MAHA BHALINGTA TEDZO BHALINGTA BHALA
BHATE GUHYA SAMAYA HUNG HRI THA

ཞེས་རེ་མ་བཞིན་ལན་གསུམ་གྱིས་སྦྱང་༔

Purify by repeating each of these three times in succession.

[The Main Visualization]

དེ་ནས་སྐད་ཅིག་དྲན་རྫོགས་སུ༔

Then, instantly recollect.

ཧཱུྃ༔   སྟོང་པའི་ངང་ལས་སྣང་སྲིད་གཞལ་ཡས་ཁང༔

HUNG   TONG PE NGANG LE NANG SI ZHAL YE KHANG

HUNG   Within emptiness, apparent existence is the
              immeasurable palace.

ཨེ་ལས་རབ་འཇིགས་པོ་འབྱུང་འབར་བའི་དབུས༔

E LE RAB JIG PO DRANG BAR WE U

From the syllable E arises the terrifying, blazing palace, which has
in its center

འཁོར་ལོ་རྩིབས་བཞི་ཆོས་འབྱུང་ཏི་རའི་དབུས༔

KHOR LO TSIB ZHI CHÖ JUNG TI RE U

A wheel with four spokes; above that is the source of dharmas,
then tiras.

རང་ཉིད་དཔལ་ཆེན་རྡོ་རྗེ་གཞོན་ནུའི་སྐུ༔

RANG NYI PAL CHEN DOR JE ZHÖN NÜ KU

On that is oneself, Great Splendor Dorje Zhönu,

མཐིང་ནག་ངམ་པ་ཞལ་གཅིག་ཕྱག་གཉིས་པ༔

TING NAG NGAM PA ZHAL CHIG CHAG NYI PA

Dark blue and awesome, with one face and two arms,

ཕྱག་གཡས་རྡོ་རྗེ་གཡོན་པས་ཕུར་པ་བསྣམས༔

CHAG YE DOR JE YÖN PE PUR PA NAM

Holding a vajra in the right hand and a phurba in the left,

སྒྲོ་གཤོག་བརྐྱངས་ཤིང་དུར་ཁྲོད་ཆས་ཀྱིས་བརྒྱན༔

DRO SHOG JANG SHING DUR TRÖ CHE CHI JEN

With feathered wings extended, and adorned with cemetery ornaments,

བརྐྱངས་བསྐུམ་ཞབས་ཀྱིས་དམ་སྲི་རུ་དྲ་མནན༔

CHANG KUM ZHAB CHI DAM SI RU DRA NEN

With one leg extended and the other slightly bent, crushing Rudra and corrupters of samaya.

འཁོར་ལོ་རྒྱས་འདེབས་གསང་ཡེ་པང་དུ་འཁྱུད༔

KHOR LO JE DEB SANG YE PANG DU CHÜ

He embraces Diptachakra, the secret wisdom consort, in his lap.

གྲི་ཐོད་མགུལ་འཁྱུད་ཞབས་གཉིས་སྐེད་ལ་འཁྲིལ༔

DRI TÖ GÜL CHÜ ZHAB NYI KE LA TRIL

Holding a hooked knife and skull cup, she embraces his neck and encircles his waist with her legs.

རུས་པའི་རྒྱན་ལྡན་བདེ་ཆེན་རྒྱས་པར་བསྒོམ༔

RÜ PE JEN DEN DE CHEN JE PAR GOM

She wears bone ornaments. Ever expanding is their great bliss.

ཡབ་ཡུམ་སྐུ་ལ་འཇིགས་བྱེད་མེ་ཕུང་འཁྲིགས༔

YAB YUM KU LA JIG JE ME PUNG TRIG

The form of the father and consort is in a terrifying mass of flames.

ལོག་འདྲེན་བདུད་བཞི་ཚར་གཅོད་དཔའ་བོར་གསལ༔

LOG DREN DÜ ZHI TSAR CHÖ PA WOR SAL

Clearly visualize the hero destroying the four demons and those who lead beings astray.

ཨོཾ་བཛྲ་ཀི་ལི་ཀི་ལ་ཡ་སརྦ་བིགྷྣན་ཏྲིག་ནན་བཾ་ཧཱུྃ་ཕཊ༔

OM VAJRA KILI KILAYA SARVA BIGHNEN TRIGNEN BAM HUNG PHET

དམིགས་པ་སྤྲོ་བསྡུ་ལ་སོགས་སྤྱི་ལྟར་བྱ༔ སྟོས་མེད་ལུགས་སུ་བསྒྲུབ་ན་མཆོད་པ་དང༔

སྟོས་པའི་དཀྱིལ་འཁོར་ལ་སོགས་མེད་པར་བྱ༔ རྟེན་འབྲེལ་ཐབས་ཚམ་སྤྲོས་པ་བྱེད་མོས་ན༔

རྟེན་འབྲེལ་ཐབས་ཚམ་

Visualize, emanate and gather, and so on, as is generally done. If you want to do the practice in a simple way, there is no need for offerings or an elaborate mandala, and so on. If you want to do it elaborately, merely as relative skillful means, combine the preliminary sections with the concluding sections just like this.

[Invoking the Jnanasattvas]

ཧཱུྃ༔ དམ་ཚིག་སེམས་དཔའི་ཐུགས་ཀའི་འོད་ཟེར་གྱིས༔

HUNG   DAM TSIG SEM PE TUG KE Ö ZER JI

HUNG   Light rays from the heart center of the samayasattva

ཡང་དག་ཡེ་ཤེས་དཔལ་ཆེན་ལྷ་ཚོགས་རྣམས༔

YANG DAG YE SHE PAL CHEN LHA TSOG NAM

Invite the perfectly pure jnanasattva, Great Splendor, and his
entire retinue.

སྤྱན་དྲངས་ཛཿཧཱུྃ་བྃ་ཧོཿས་གཉིས་མེད་བསྟིམ༔

CHEN DRANG DZA HUNG BAM HO NYI ME TIM

With DZA HUNG BAM HO, they dissolve inseparably.

བདག་ལ་དབང་བསྐུར་བྱིན་བརླབས་བརྟན་པར་བཞུགས༔

DAG LA WANG KUR JIN LAB TEN PAR ZHUG

Please grant the empowerment and blessings, and stabilize them.

དུག་ལྔ་རྣམ་དག་ཕྱི་ནང་མཆོད་པ་འབུལ༔

DUG NGA NAM DAG CHI NANG CHÖ PA BÜL

I offer the fully purified five poisons and the outer and inner
offerings.

སྐུ་གསུང་ཐུགས་མཆོག་དངོས་གྲུབ་སྩལ་ཏུ་གསོལ༔

KU SUNG TUG CHOG NGÖ DRUB TSAL TU SÖL

Please bestow the supreme siddhi of body, speech, and mind.

ཨོཾ་བཛྲ་ས་མ་ཡ་ཏིཥྛ་ལྷེན༔

OM VAJRA SAMAYA TISHTHA LHEN

ཨ་བེ་ཤ་ཡ་ཨ་བྷི་ཥི་ཉྩ་ཧཱུྃ༔

AVESHAYA ABHISHINYETSA HUNG

ཨོཾ་བཛྲ་པུཥྤེ་དྷུ་པེ་ཨ་ལོ་ཀེ་གནྡྷེ་ནཻ་ཝི་ད་བ་ཤ་བྡ་ཨཱ༔ཧཱུྃ༔

OM VAJRA PUSHPE DHUPE ALOKE GANDHE NAIVIDYA
SHABDA AH HUNG

ཨོཾ་སརྦ་པ་ཉྩ་ཨ་མྲྀ་ཏ་ར་ཀྟ་བྷ་ལིཾ་ཏ་ཁ་ཧི༔

OM SARVA PENYETSA AMRITA RAKTA BHALINGTA
KHA HI

The Praise

ཧཱུྃ༔ མ་བཅོས་ལྷུན་གྲུབ་རྡོ་རྗེ་གཞོན་ནུའི་དཔལ༔

HUNG   MA CHÖ LHÜN DRUB DOR JE ZHÖN NÜ PAL
HUNG   Unfabricated, spontaneous, glorious Dorje Zhönu,

སྐུ་ཡི་རྒྱན་རྫོགས་གར་དགུས་ས་གསུམ་གཡོ༔

KU YI JEN DZOG GAR GÜ SA SUM YO
Your body with the nine gestures, perfectly adorned, shakes the
three grounds.

གསུང་གི་ཧཱུྃ་སྒྲའི་དྲག་སྔགས་འབྲུག་ལྟར་སྒྲོགས༔

SUNG GI HUNG DRE DRAG NGAG DRUG TAR DROG
Your speech, the wrathful mantra of HUNG, roars like thunder.

ཕྱགས་མཆོག་མི་གཡོ་ཡང་དག་འཁོར་ལོའི་གཏེར༔

TUG CHOG MI YO YANG DAG KHOR LÖ TER

Your mind, supreme and unshakable, is the treasure of the completely pure mandala.

བདེ་ཆེན་རང་བཞིན་ཟུང་འཇུག་ཧེ་རུ་ཀ༔

DE CHEN RANG ZHIN ZUNG JUG HE RU KA

Union of great bliss and true nature, Heruka,

འཇིགས་བྱེད་ཁྲོ་རྒྱལ་ཡབ་ཡུམ་སྐུ་ལ་བསྟོད༔

JIG JE TRO JAL YAB YUM KU LA TÖ

I praise the form of the terrifying, wrathful, and victorious father and consort.

ཨོཾ་བཛྲ་ཀཱི་ལི་ཀཱི་ལ་ཡ་སརྦ་བིགྷྣན་ཏྲིགྣན་བཾ་ཧཱུྃ་ཕཊ༔

OM VAJRA KILI KILAYA SARVA BIGHNEN TRIGNEN BAM HUNG PHET

དབང་བླང་བ་ནི༔

Receiving the Empowerments

ཧཱུྃ༔ གདོད་ནས་ལྷན་སྐྱེས་རྡོ་རྗེ་གཞོན་ནུའི་སྐུ༔

HUNG   DÖ NE LHEN CHE DOR JE ZHÖN NÜ KU

HUNG   The form of Dorje Zhönu, primordially coemergent,

ལྔ་ལྡན་ཡེ་ཤེས་བྱིན་རླབས་ནུས་མཐུ་ཡིས༔

NGA DEN YE SHE JIN LAB NÜ TU YI

Has the power to confer the blessings of the five wisdoms.

སྐལ་ལྡན་བདག་ལ་དབང་བསྐུར་རྒྱུད་སྨིན་ཏེ༔

KAL DEN DAG LA WANG KUR JÜ MIN TE

Please empower me, a fortunate one, and ripen my being.

མཆོག་ཐུན་འབྲས་བུ་ཡོངས་རྫོགས་དངོས་གྲུབ་སྩོལ༔

CHOG TÜN DRE BU YONG DZOG NGÖ DRUB TSÖL

Grant the complete fruition of the ordinary and supreme siddhis.

ༀ་བཛྲ་ཀུ་མཱ་ར་བཾ་ཌཱ་ཀི་ནི་ཧཱུྃ༔

OM VAJRA KUMARA BAM DAKINI HUNG

ཀཱ་ཡ་ཝཱཀ་ཙིཏྟ་སིདྡྷི་ཧཱུྃ༔

KAYA WAKA TSITTA SIDDHI HUNG

རྫོགས་རིམ་ནི༔

The Completion Stage

ཧཱུྃ༔ མི་དམིགས་དཀྱིལ་འཁོར་ཀ་དག་དབྱིངས༔

HUNG   MI MIG CHIL KHOR KA DAG YING

HUNG   Dissolve into the perfectly pure space, the mandala
beyond thought,

རང་བཞིན་ཡེ་ཤེས་ཀློང་དུ་ཧོ༔

RANG ZHIN YE SHE LONG DU HO

The vast expanse of self-existing wisdom. HO!

ཨ་ཨ་ཨ༔

A   A   A

བསྔོ་སྨོན་ནི༔

Dedication and Aspiration Prayers

རྣམ་དཀར་དགེ་ཚོགས་རྒྱ་མཚོ་ཉིད༔

NAM KAR GE TSOG JA TSO NYI
I dedicate the vast accumulation of completely pure virtue

མཐའ་ཡས་སངས་རྒྱས་ཐོབ་ཕྱིར་བསྔོ༔

TA YE SANG JE TOB CHIR NGO
So that limitless sentient beings may attain enlightenment.

བདེ་དགེ་མཆོག་གསུམ་འདུས་པ་ཡི༔

DE GE CHOG SUM DÜ PA YI
Embodiment of the happiness and goodness of the three jewels,

ཐུགས་རྗེའི་སྨོན་ལམ་དེང་འགྲུབ་ཤོག༔

TUG JE MÖN LAM DENG DRUB SHOG
May your compassionate aspiration be fulfilled at this time.

The Dependent Relations Mantra

OM YE DHARMA HETU PRABAWA HETÜNTESHAN
TATHAGATO HAYAWADAT TESHANCHA YO NIRODA
EWAM WADI MAHA SHRAMA NAYE SWAHA

བཀྲ་ཤིས་ནི༔

Prayer of Auspiciousness

ཧཱུྃ༔ ཆོས་དབྱིངས་ཀློང་དགུའི་གཏེར་ཆེན་ཇི༔

HUNG CHÖ YING LONG GÜ TER CHEN JI

HUNG The great treasure of the nine spaces of dharmadhatu

ཟབ་རྒྱས་འགྲོ་ཀུན་སྨིན་མཛད་པ༔

ZAB JE DRO KÜN MIN DZE PA

Ripens all sentient beings by profound and vast activities.

དེང་འདིར་བཀྲ་ཤིས་བདེ་ལེགས་ཤོག༔

DENG DIR TA SHI DE LEG SHOG

At this time, may there be auspiciousness and happiness.

ཞེས་དབང་བླང་ཞིང་དམིགས་པ་སྒོ་བསྒྱུའི་དང་ནས་རང་ལ་བསྟིམ༔ ས་མ་ཡ༔ ཨེ་མ༔

ཟབ་པའི་ཡང་སྙིང་དཔའ་བོ་གཅིག་སྒྲུབ་ཀྱི༔ མན་ངག་གནད་མས་པ་སྙིང་གི་ཐིག་ལེ་བཤག༔

ལས་ཅན་ཕུགས་ཀྱི་སྲས་དང་འཕྲད་པར་ཤོག༔

ཐ་ཚེ་ཁ་ཐམ༔ གཏེར་རྒྱ༔ སྦས་རྒྱ༔ ཟབ་རྒྱ༔ གསང་རྒྱ༔ གཏད་རྒྱ༔

Having received initiation and done the visualizing, emanating, and gathering, dissolve into oneself. **SAMAYA**

E MA   For the practice of the ekavira, the very essence of profundity,
I have presented here the heart essence of the oral instructions.
May a karmically connected heart son find this.
Treasure seal. Hidden seal. Profound seal. Secret seal.
Pointing-out seal.

བོ་བོ་ཨོ་རྒྱན་རྩ་གསུམ་གླིང་པ་ཆོས་ཀྱི་རྒྱ་མཚོས་མེ་སྤྲེལ་ལོར་མོན་ཤ་འུག་སྟག་སྒོ་ནས་གདན་
དྲངས་ཞིང་གསང་སྔགས་ཆོས་གླིང་དུ་ཤོག་སེར་ལས་ཞལ་བཤུས་སོ།།

I, Orgyen Tsasum Lingpa Chökyi Gyatso, in the Fire Monkey year, took this from Mön Sha'ug Taggo and transcribed from yellow parchment at Sang-ngag Chöling.

This translation was prepared by Ven. Khenchen Palden Sherab Rinpoche, Ven. Khenpo Tsewang Dongyal Rinpoche and Steve Sheldon in 1985. It was revised and reprinted for Dharma Samudra in 1991 with help from Lama Ugyen Shenpen, Tony Duff, Steve Harris, Ann Helm, Nancy Roberts, Carl Stuendel, and Gerry Wiener.

བླ་མེད་ཡང་ཕུར་གྲུ་འུ་དམར་ནག་ལས༔

From The Dark Red Amulet
of Unsurpassable Yang-Phur

སྟོབས་ལྡན་ཕུར་པ་ནག་པོའི་ཧཱུྃ་སྒྲུབ་བཞུགས་སོ༔

THE PRACTICE OF THE HUNG OF THE
POWERFUL BLACK PHURBA

ཨོ་རྒྱན་རྩ་གསུམ་གླིང་པ་ཆོས་ཀྱི་རྒྱ་མཚོས་གཏེར་མའོ།།

Orgyen Tsasum Lingpa Chökyi Gyatso

By practicing on this may all sentient beings
achieve the perfect true-nature state of the lama.
May their highest aspiration be fulfilled
for the benefit of all sentient beings.

ཨོཾ༔ སྟིཝྲ་ཏྲ༔ དཔལ་ཆེན་ཧེ་རུ་ཀ་ལ་འདུད༔ ས་མ་ཡ༔ ཕུ་སྲ་ཏཱ༔

ཨེ་མ་རྩལ་ཆེན་སྟོབས་འབྱིན་པ༔ ཡང་ཕུར་ནག་པོའི་སྒྲུབ་པ་འདི༔

ཀུན་གྱིས་ཐུན་མོང་མ་ཡིན་ཟབ༔ ཁྱད་པར་བན་བོན་སྔགས་པ་དང༔

ལྷ་སྲིན་འབྱུང་པོ་གདུག་ཅན་གྱིས༔ བར་ཆོད་འཚེ་བ་ལྡང་གྱུར་ན༔

དེ་ཚེ་འདི་ཉིད་ཤིན་ཏུ་གཅེས༔ སྤྲོས་མེད་སྒྲུབ་པ་ཁྱད་མཆོག་གོ༔ ས་མ་ཡ༔

Homage to Great Splendor Heruka.   **SAMAYA**
E MA *Producing the power of great energy,*
This practice of the **HUNG** *of the black Yang-Phur*
Is not a general practice; it is profound.
In particular, when from evil Buddhists, Bönpos, mantra practitioners, and
Gods, rakshas, and spirits
Obstacles and harm arise,
This practice is very important.
Without elaboration, this practice is particularly supreme.
SAMAYA

དང་པོ་དྲན་རྟོགས་ལྷ་བསྐྱེད་ནི༔

First, instantly recollect and visualize the deity.

ཧཱུྂ་ཧཱུྂ་ཧཱུྂ༔

HUNG HUNG HUNG

བདག་ཉིད་དཔལ་ཆེན་ཧེ་རུ་ཀ༔

DAG NYI PAL CHEN HE RU KA

I myself am Great Splendor Heruka.

འཇིགས་བྱེད་རྡོ་རྗེ་གཞོན་ནུའི་སྐུ༔

JIG JE DOR JE ZHÖN NÜ KU

The terrifying form of Dorje Zhönu

ཁམ་ནག་ཞལ་གསུམ་ཕྱག་དྲུག་པ༔

KHAM NAG ZHAL SUM CHAG DRUG PA

Is dark brown, with three faces and six arms,

ཁྲོ་གཏུམ་ཚ་ཚ་སྐར་ལྟར་འཁྲུགས༔

TRO TUM TSA TSA KAR TAR TRUG

And wrathful, dazzling with sparks like shooting stars.

གཡས་གཉིས་གནམ་ལྕགས་རྡོ་རྗེ་ཡིས༔

YE NYI NAM CHAG DOR JE YI

The two upper right hands hold vajras of meteoric iron,

མ་རུང་གདུག་པའི་བན་བོན་གཞོམ༔

MA RUNG DUG PE BEN BÖN ZHOM

Which destroy cruel and evil Buddhists and Bönpos.

གཡོན་གཉིས་མེ་ཕུང་ཁ་ཊྭཱཾ་གིས༔

YÖN NYI ME PUNG KHATVANG GI

The two upper left hands hold flames of fire and a khatvanga,

སྡེ་བརྒྱད་འབྱུང་པོའི་སྲོག་སྙིང་ཕྲལ༔

DE JE JUNG PÖ SOG NYING TRAL

Which cut off the life force of the eight classes of spirits.

མཐའ་གཉིས་རི་རབ་ཕུར་པ་ཡིས༔

TA NYI RI RAB PUR PA YI

The lowest two hands hold a mountainlike phurba,

རྒྱལ་བསེན་འགོང་པོ་དུལ་དུ་རློག༔

JAL SEN GONG PO DÜL DU LOG

Which crushes male and female samaya corrupters into dust.

སྒྲོ་གཤོག་སྤུ་གྲི་བརྒྱངས་པ་ཡིས༔

DRO SHOG PU TRI JANG PA YI

The wings, like outstretched razor knives,

སྣང་སྲིད་ཀུན་གྱིས་ཆོ་འཕྲུལ་བློག༔

NANG SI KÜN JI CHO TRÜL DOG

Expel the magical display of all apparent existence.

འཇིགས་པའི་དུར་ཁྲོད་ཆས་བརྒྱད་ཀྱིས༔

JIG PE DUR TRÖ CHE JE CHI

The eight terrifying charnel ground garments

ཡེ་ཤེས་འཇིག་རྟེན་ཟིལ་གྱིས་གནོན༔

YE SHE JIG TEN ZIL JI NÖN

Overpower wisdom beings and worldly beings.

 སྤྱི་བར་ཆུ་སྲིན་ངམ་ཞལ་གྱིས༔

TE WAR CHU SIN NGAM ZHAL JI

The mouth of an awesome, powerful crocodile at the navel

དམ་སྲི་འདྲེ་རྒོད་སྙིང་ཁྲག་རོལ༔

DAM SI DRE GÖ NYING TRAG RÖL

Drinks the heart blood of the evil spirits who corrupt samaya.

སྐུ་སྨད་གནམ་ལྕགས་ཕུར་གཤམ་གྱིས༔

KU ME NAM CHAG PUR SHAM JI

The lower body, shaped like the blade of a meteoric iron phurba,

སྟོང་ཁམས་རུ་དྲའི་སྲོག་དབུགས་ཕྲལ༔

TONG KHAM RU DRE SOG UG TRAL

Cuts off the life breath of the rudras of the three realms.

སྐུ་ལ་མེ་ཕུང་འཕྲིགས་པ་ཡིས༔

KU LA ME PUNG TRIG PA YI

Around the body, a mass of flames

ལོག་འདྲེན་བདུད་བཞིའི་དཔུང་ཚོགས་བསྲེགས༔

LOG DREN DÜ ZHI PUNG TSOG SEG

Burns the troops of the four demons and those who lead
beings astray.

ཡུམ་ཆེན་འཁོར་ལོ་རྒྱས་འདེབས་འཁྲིལ༔

YUM CHEN KHOR LO JE DEB TRIL

Embracing the great mother, Diptachakra,

ཁྲོ་རྒྱལ་སྟོབས་ལྡན་ཀི་ལ་ཡ༔

TRO JAL TOB DEN KILAYA

The wrathful king, powerful Kilaya,

བདུད་འདུལ་དཔལ་གྱི་སྐུ་རུ་ཤར༔

DÜ DÜL PAL JI KU RU SHAR

Appears in a glorious form that subdues demons.

དབང་སྡུད་ཟིལ་གནོན་ལྷུན་གྱིས་གྲུབ༔

WANG DÜ ZIL NÖN LHÜN JI DRUB

With the power of subjugation, spontaneously overwhelming,

བདུད་དགྲ་ཚར་གཅོད་ལས་གྲུབ་གྱུར༔

DÜ DRA TSAR CHÖ LE DRUB JUR

The action of annihilating hostile demons is accomplished.

ཧཱུྃ་ཧཱུྃ་ཧཱུྃ༔

HUNG HUNG HUNG

ཧཱུྃ་ཧཱུྃ་ཧཱུྃ༔

HUNG HUNG HUNG

ཧཱུྃ་ཧཱུྃ་ཧཱུྃ་ཧཱུྃ༔

HUNG HUNG HUNG HUNG

གྲགས་སྟོང་དང་དུ་ཅི་ནུས་བཟླས༔

In the state of sound-emptiness, recite this for as long as possible.

187

ས་མ་ཡཿ ཨེ་མ་ཟབ་པའི་མཐར་ཕྱུག་ལསཿ ཡང་ཟབ་ཧཱུྃ་གི་སྒྲུབ་ཐབས་བཞགཿ

མ་འོངས་དུས་ཀྱི་ཐ་མ་རུཿ སྙུགས་ཀྱི་སྲས་དང་འཕྲད་པར་ཤོགཿ ས་མ་ཡཿ

རྒྱ་རྒྱ་རྒྱཿ གཏེར་རྒྱཿ སྦས་རྒྱཿ ཟབ་རྒྱཿ གསང་རྒྱཿ གཏད་རྒྱཿ

SAMAYA
E MA   Of the utmost profundity,
This sadhana of the HUNG was presented
For the future dark age.
May a heart son find this.   SAMAYA
Treasure seal. Hidden seal. Profound Seal. Secret seal. Pointing-out seal.

ཨོ་རྒྱན་རྩ་གསུམ་གླིང་པ་ཆོས་ཀྱི་རྒྱ་མཚོས་མེ་སྤྲེལ་ལོར་མོན་ཤ་འུག་སྟག་སྒོ་ནས་གདན་

དྲངས་སྤས་ཡུལ་གསང་སྔགས་ཆོས་གླིང་དུ་ཤོག་སེར་ལས་ལེགས་པར་བཤུས་པའོ།།

I, Orgyen Tsasum Lingpa Chökyi Gyatso, in the Fire Monkey year, took
this from Mön Sha'ug Taggo, and transcribed it correctly from yellow
parchment at Beyul Sang-ngak Chöling.

This translation was prepared by Venerable Khenchen Palden Sherab
Rinpoche, Venerable Khenpo Tsewang Dongyal Rinpoche, and Steve
Sheldon in 1995. It was revised and reprinted for Dharma Samudra in
1991 with help from Lama Ugyen Shenpen, Tony Duff, Steve Harris,
Ann Helm, Nancy Roberts, Carl Stuendel, and Gerry Wiener.

THE SANSKRIT VOWELS AND CONSONANTS

OM	A	AH	I	II
	U	UU	RI	RII
	LI	LII	AY	AYY
	O	AU	ANG	AH
KA	KHA	GA	GHA	NGA
TSA	TSHA	DZA	DZHA	NYA
TA	THA	DA	DHA	NA
TA	THA	DA	DHA	NA
PA	PHA	BA	BHA	MA
YA	RA	LA	WA	
SHA	KHA	SA	HA	JA

THE VAJRASATTVA MANTRA

ༀ་བཛྲ་སཏྭ་ས་མ་ཡ་མ་ནུ་པཱ་ལ་ཡཿ

OM VAJRASATTVA SAMAYA MANU PALA YA

བཛྲ་སཏྭ་ཏེ་ནོ་པཿ

VAJRASATTVA TENO PA

ཏིཥྛ་དྲྀཌྷོ་མེ་བྷ་ཝཿ

TISHTHA DRIDHO ME BHAWA

སུ་ཏོ་ཥྱོ་མེ་བྷ་ཝཿ

SUTO KAYO ME BHAWA

སུ་པོ་ཥྱོ་མེ་བྷ་ཝཿ

SUPO KAYO ME BHAWA

ཨ་ནུ་རཀྟོ་མེ་བྷ་ཝཿ

ANU RAKTO ME BHAWA

སརྦ་སིདྡྷི་མེ་པྲ་ཡཙྪཿ

SARVA SIDDHIM ME PRAYATTSA

སརྦ་ཀརྨ་སུ་ཙ་མེཿ

SARVA KARMA SUTSA ME

ཙིཏྟཾ་ཤྲེ་ཡཾ་ཀུ་རུ་ཧཱུྃཿ

TSITTAM SHREYAM KURU HUNG

ཧ་ཧ་ཧ་ཧ་ཧོཿ ་ བྷ་ག་ཝནཿ

HA HA HA HA HO   BHAGAWAN

སརྦ་ཏ་ཐཱ་ག་ཏ་བཛྲ་མ་མེ་མུཉྩཿ

SARVA TATHAGATA VAJRA MAME MÜNTSA

བཛྲི་བྷ་ཝ་མ་ཧཱ་ས་མ་ཡ་སཏྭ་ཨཿ

VAJRI BHAWA MAHA SAMAYA SATTVA AH

THE DEPENDENT RELATIONS MANTRA

ༀ་ཡེ་དྷརྨ་ཧེ་ཏུ

OM YE DHARMA HETU

པྲ་བྷ་ཝ་ཧེ་ཏུནྟེ་ཤན་

PRABAWA HETÜNTESHAN

ཏ་ཐཱ་ག་ཏོ་ཧྱ་བ་དཏ་

TATHAGATO HAYAWADAT

ཏེ་ཥཱཉྩ་ཡོ་ནི་རོ་དྷ་

TESHANCHA YO NIRODA

ཨེ་ཝཾ་བ་དི་མ་ཧཱ་ཤྲ་མ་ཎ་ཡེ་སྭ་ཧཱཿ

EWAM WADI MAHA SHRAMA NAYE SWAHA

Notes

1. These are terma teachings of the great tertön Drikung Rinchen Phuntsok of the Drikung Kagyu lingeage.

2. Rigdzin Thugchog Dorje, an emanation of Hungkara, one of the Eight Great Vidyadharas (see note 15), was a great tertön who revealed many termas and was one of the principal teachers of Rigdzin Jigme Lingpa. As a lineage holder of Tsasum Lingpa, Rigdzin Thugchog Dorje edited his terma teachings and transmitted them to many students.

3. This refers to the Fire Dog year of 1726.

4. Empowerment is *abhisheka* in Sanskrit and *dbang* in Tibetan.

5. This is the pure land of Vajrakilaya, *gsang chen me ri 'bar ba.*

6. *byang chub kyi sems kun byed rgyal po*

7. *rdo rje phur pa* and *rdo rje gzhon nu*

8. This is the *Supreme Awareness Tantra, rig pa mchog gi spyi rgyud.* This Vajrakilaya tantra is divided into different groups, such as the root tantra, the trunk tantra, the branch tantra, the leaf tantra, the flower tantra, and the fruit tantra.

9. *phur pa gsang ba'i rgyud*

10. *phur pa mya ngan las 'das pa'i rgyud*

11. *rdor rje khros pa rtza ba'i rgyud*

12. *ki la ya bcu gnyis rgyud*

13. Nam Chag Barwa, the "meteorite" mountain (sometimes referred to as Sri Pad Mountain), is located in present-day Sri Lanka.

14. This is a very famous stupa that was located in the charnel ground called Sitavan ("Cool Grove") near Bodhgaya, India.

15. The Eight Great Vidyadharas are Manjushrimitra, Nagarjuna, Hungkara, Vimalamitra, Prabhahasti, Dhanasamskrita, Rombuguhya, and Shantigarbha (if we include Guru Padmasambhava, there are Nine Great Vidyadharas).

16. *'jam dpal gsang ba'i rgyud*

17. *rta mchog rol pa rtza ba'i rgyud*

18. *dpal chen he ru ka'i rgyud*

19. *rgyud lung 'bum tig rgyud*

20. *rgyud thams cad kyi rgyal po*

21. *dmod pa drag sngags kyi rgyud*

22. *bde gshegs 'dus pa'i rgyud*

23. Many great masters of the Vajrakilaya lineage, such as Guru Padmasambhava, Prabhahasti, and Vimalamitra, were originally from India.

24. *bla ma rig 'dzin rgyud*

25. Yangleshöd is known as a very famous historic place of Vajrakilaya. It is located in present-day Pharping in Nepal.

26. The nine lamps, *yang dag mar me dgu pa,* are symbols of the mandala.

27. Mahamudra is also known as *lhun grub rig 'dzin,* the "spontaneous vidyadhara state."

28. Mount Shilgongdrag is in the Khargong area of Nepal.

29. *phur pa 'bum nag*

30. *ma mo rbod gtong*

31. *'jig rten mchod bstod*

32. See note 21.

33. *mon kha ne'u ring seng ge rdzongs*

34. *mdo 'grel mun pa'i go cha*

35. *bsam gtan mig sgron*

36. This is the pure land of Guru Rinpoche, *zangs mdog dpal ri.*

37. In Tibet there are five great mountains said to symbolize the body, speech, mind, quality, and activity aspects of the buddhas. Jowo Zegyal represents the quality aspect.

38. Tsampa is roasted barley flour, a staple of the traditional Tibetan diet, to which butter and tea are added.

39. The mountain of Ahmye Mutri (*aa mye mu khri*) is about sixty miles south of Tsasum Lingpa's monastery.

40. The ratna family is the jewel family, located in the southern direction of the mandala.

41. Öser Chang is the name of one of the ancient great dakinis.

42. Pema Kö (*padma bkod*) is the "hidden land" at the confluence of the Tsangpo and Brahmaputra rivers in Tibet, north of the border with Assam, India.

43. Kön Chog Chidu (*dkon mchog sryi 'dus*) is the condensed three-roots tsok practice.

44. A khatvanga is a trident-shaped ritual implement with various kinds of ornamentation.

45. *mu men*, lapis lazuli

46. Mön Sha'ug Taggo, which is very far from Lhasa, is close to Assam at the border with India.

47. Gaus, even larger ones, are meant to be wearable and used as portable shrines with holy objects (*byun rten bshog*) inside such as a Buddha statue or image, blessed medicine, relics, and so forth.

48. *nyi zla kha sbyor gyi rgyud*

49. *dbu ma rtsa ba shes rab*

50. *rnam snang mngon byang gi rgyud*

51. *phur pa'i rgyud*

52. The garuda is a wisdom being known as the "king of the birds" and depicted in thangkas holding a snake in its beak. According to Hindu tradition, Vishnu rides upon a garuda.

53. *dbu ma la 'jug pa*

54. *gnam lcags*

55. *shes rab kyi pha rol tu phyin pa'i mdo*

56. *gsang ba snying po'i rgyud,* "the secret essence tantra"

57. *mngon rtogs rgyan*

58. *dus kyi 'khor lo'i rgyud*

59. *rig pa mchog gi rgyud [chen po]*

60. Ra Lotsawa was a great scholar of the new translation schools of Tibetan Buddhism.

Glossary of Sanskrit in the Mantras

ABHISHINYETSA empowerment, initiation; also ABHISHEKA

AH speech aspect of the buddhas

AH KARSHA YA come here instantly

ALOKE light

AMRITA nectar of wisdom

AVESHAYA invoking

BAM confirming

BAM DAKINI refers to the consort; BAM (joy) is the seed syllable of the dakini.

BHALA BHATE mighty one, powerful one

BHALINGTA torma

BIGHNEN demons

DHUPE incense

DZA invoking

DZOLA glorious, flaming, erupting

E great emptiness

GANDHE perfumed water

GUHYA secret

HO joy

HUNG mingling or connecting; requesting insistently; invoking primordial wisdom; the five wisdoms and the five kayas; the mind aspect of the buddhas

KALAKSHA vase

KAYA body

KHAHI enjoy; have a good appetite

KHAM water

KILAYA phurba, a three-bladed dagger with a single point
KUMARA youthful
MAHA great
MANDALA mandala
NAIVIDYA food
NAMO an expression of joyful and devoted feeling
OM auspiciousness; the body aspect of the buddhas
PENYETSA five
PHET cut thoroughly
PUSHPE flower
RAKSHA protection
RAKTA red
RAM fire
RUDRA demon
SAMAYA spiritual connection
SARVA all
SATTVA courageous one, being
SHABDA music
SIDDHI accomplishment
SWAHA establish
TAKI RADZA the king of passion
TEDZO glorious
TISHTHA LHEN remain firmly
TRAYA three
TRIGNEN nail
TSINDHA cut thoroughly
TSITTA mind
VAJRA indestructible, stable, condensed
WAKA speech
WIDHO awareness
YAM wind
YE within

Tibetan Glossary

dorje (vajra); rdo rje—diamondlike scepter; indestructible nature

dze; rdzas—substance; objects; symbolic substantial phurba is mtshan ma rdzas kyi phur pa.

Dzogchen; rdzogs chen—Great Perfection (rdzogs pa chen po) teachings and practice

gau; ga'u—locket or amulet that symbolizes the union of skillful means and wisdom, appearance and emptiness; may hold secret terma teachings and be worn as a portable shrine.

gyaltsen; rgyal btsan—gyalpo and tsenmo; male and female demons

jangchub sem (bodhichitta); byang chub sems—enlightenment mind; vast motivation of great compassion, loving-kindness, and wisdom

kadag; ka dag—pure from the beginning

khandro (dakini); mkha' 'gro—sky dancer; female wisdom being

kunzhi (alaya); kun gzhi—all-ground; the source of all conditioned habitual patterns and all pure vision

lama (guru); blama—teacher; spiritual friend

lhündrub; lhun grub—spontaneous presence

lung; rlung—wind energy; winds

nyi dzin; gnyis 'dzin—duality clinging

nyingje; snying rje—compassion

Ogmin (Akanishta); 'og min—the pure land beyond all dualistic concepts

pecha; dpe cha—Tibetan text in unbound, long pages

phurba (kilaya); phur pa—three-bladed dagger with a single point

rigdzin; rig 'dzin—vidyadhara; holder of awareness; one who is highly realized rigpa; rig pa—awareness

sangye; sangs rgyas—buddha

sung khor; srung 'khor—protection wheel or boundary

terma; gter ma—secret treasure teachings hidden by Guru Padmasambhava and Yeshe Tsogyal and revealed by the tertön connected
with those teachings

tertön; gter ston—treasure revealer

thigle; thig le—essence element of the body; energy

tögal; thod rgal—jumping or leaping over (*see also* trekchö)

tonglen; tong len—the exchanging practice of giving and taking; sending
one's happiness to others and receiving their suffering

trekchö; khreg gcod—cutting thoroughly; essence practice (with tögal) of
Dzogchen

tsa; rtsa—channels; tsa lung practice involves working with the channels
and wind energy of the body.

tsenma; mtshan ma—symbol; characteristic

tummo; gtum mo—practice of the yoga of inner or psychic heat; literally,
"cruel lady"

wang (abhisheka); dbang—empowerment

yeshe; ye shes—wisdom

ying (dhatu); dbyings—the natural state; chos kyi dbyings or
dharmadhatu is the nature of all phenomena.

zhönu (kumara); gzhon nu—very youthful; another name for Vajrakilaya
is Dorje Zhönu

LIST OF

Photographs & Illustrations

About the Authors

KHENCHEN PALDEN SHERAB RINPOCHE

Venerable Khenchen Palden Sherab Rinpoche is a renowned scholar and meditation master of Nyingma, the Ancient School of Tibetan Buddhism. He was born on May 10, 1942 in the Dhoshul region of Kham, eastern Tibet, near the sacred mountain Jowo Zegyal. On the morning of his birth a small snow fell with the flakes in the shape of lotus petals. Among his ancestors were many great scholars, practitioners, and treasure revealers.

His family was semi-nomadic, living in the village during the winter and moving with the herds to high mountain pastures where they lived in yak hair tents during the summers. The monastery for the Dhoshul region is called Gochen and his father's family had the hereditary responsibility for administration of the business affairs of the monastery. His grandfather had been both administrator and chantmaster in charge of the ritual ceremonies.

He started his education at the age of four at Gochen Monastery, which was founded by Tsasum Lingpa. At the age of twelve he entered Riwoche Monastery and completed his studies just before the Chinese invasion of Tibet reached that area. His root teacher was the illustrious Khenpo Tenzin Dragpa (Katog Khenpo Akshu).

In 1960, Rinpoche and his family were forced into exile, escaping to India. Eventually in 1967 he was appointed head of the Nyingma department of the Central Institute of Higher Tibetan Studies in Sarnath by His Holiness Dudjom Rinpoche, the Supreme Head of the Nyingma School of Tibetan Buddhism. He held this position for seventeen years, as an abbot, dedicating all his time and energy to ensure the survival and spread of the Buddhist teachings.

Rinpoche moved to the United States in 1984 to work closely with H.H. Dudjom Rinpoche. In 1985, Venerable Khenchen Palden Sherab Rinpoche and his brother Venerable Khenpo Tsewang Dongyal Rinpoche founded the Dharma Samudra Publishing Company. In 1988, they founded the Padmasambhava Buddhist Center, which has centers throughout the United States, as well as in Puerto Rico, Russia, and India. The primary center is Padma Samye Ling, located in Delaware County, New York. Padmasambhava Buddhist Center also includes a traditional Tibetan Buddhist monastery and nunnery at the holy site of Deer Park in Sarnath and the Miracle Stupa at Padma Samye Jetavan in Jetavan Grove, Shravasti, India.

Rinpoche travels extensively within the United States and throughout the world, giving teachings and empowerments at numerous retreats and seminars, in addition to establishing meditation centers.

His three volumes of collected works in Tibetan include:

Opening the Eyes of Wisdom, a commentary on Sangye Yeshe's *Lamp of the Eye of Contemplation;*

Waves of the Ocean of Devotion, a biography-praise to Nubchen Sangye Yeshe, and *Vajra Rosary*, biographies of his main incarnations;

The Mirror of Mindfulness, an explanation of the six bardos;

Advice from the Ancestral Vidyadhara, a commentary on Padmasambhava's *Stages of the Path, Heap of Jewels;*

Blazing Clouds of Wisdom and Compassion, a commentary on the hundred-syllable mantra of Vajrasattva;

The Ornament of Vairochana's Intention, a commentary on the
  Heart Sutra;
Opening the Door of Blessings, a biography of Machig Labdron;
Lotus Necklace of Devotion, a biography of Khenchen Tenzin Dragpa;
The Essence of Diamond Clear Light, an outline and structural analysis
  of *The Aspiration Prayer of Samantabhadra*;
The Lamp of Blazing Sun and Moon, a commentary on Mipham's
  Wisdom Sword;
The Ornament of Stars at Dawn, an outline and structural analysis of
  Vasubandhu's *Twenty Verses*;
Pleasure Lake of Nagarjuna's Intention, general summary of
  Madhyamaka;
Supreme Clear Mirror, an introduction to Buddhist logic;
White Lotus, an explanation of prayers to Guru Rinpoche;
Smiling Red Lotus, short commentary on the prayer to Yeshe Tsogyal;
Clouds of Blessings; an explanation of prayers to Terchen Tsasum Lingpa;
  and other learned works, poems, prayers, and sadhanas.
*The Smile of Sun and Moon: A Commentary on the Praise to the
  Twenty-One Taras.*

KHENPO TSEWANG DONGYAL RINPOCHE

Venerable Khenpo Tsewang Dongyal Rinpoche was born in the Dhoshul region of Kham in eastern Tibet on June 10, 1950. On that summer day in the family tent, Rinpoche's birth caused his mother no pain. The next day, his mother, Pema Lhadze, moved the bed where she had given birth. Beneath it she found growing a beautiful and fragrant flower which she plucked and offered to Chenrezig on the family altar.

Soon after his birth three head lamas from Jadchag Monastery came to his home and recognized him as the reincarnation of Khenpo Sherab Khyentse. Khenpo Sherab Khyentse, who had been the former head abbot lama at Gochen Monastery, was a renowned scholar and practitioner who spent much of his life in retreat.

Rinpoche's first dharma teacher was his father, Lama Chimed Namgyal Rinpoche. Beginning his schooling at the age of five, he entered Gochen Monastery. His studies were interrupted by the Chinese invasion and his family's escape to India. In India his father and brother continued his education until he entered the Nyingmapa Monastic School of northern India, where he studied until 1967. He then entered the Central Institute of Higher Tibetan Studies, which was then a part of Sanskrit University in Varanasi, where he received his B.A. degree in 1975. He also attended Nyingmapa University in West Bengal, where he received another B.A. and an M.A. in 1977.

In 1978, Rinpoche was enthroned as the abbot of the Wish-Fulfilling Nyingmapa Institute in Boudanath, Nepal by H.H. Dudjom Rinpoche, where he taught poetry, grammar, and philosophy. In 1981, H.H. Dudjom Rinpoche appointed Rinpoche as the abbot of the Dorje Nyingpo center in

Paris, France. In 1982 he was asked to work with H.H. Dudjom Rinpoche at the Yeshe Nyingpo center in New York. During the 1980s, until H.H. Dudjom Rinpoche's mahaparinirvana in 1987, Rinpoche continued working closely with H.H. Dudjom Rinpoche, often traveling with him as his translator and attendant.

In 1988, Rinpoche and his brother founded the Padmasambhava Buddhist Center. Since that time he has served as a spiritual director at the various Padmasambhava centers throughout the world. He maintains an active traveling and teaching schedule with his brother Khenchen Palden Sherab Rinpoche.

Khenpo Tsewang Rinpoche is the author of *Light of Fearless Indestructible Wisdom: The Life and Legacy of His Holiness Dudjom Rinpoche*, published in both Tibetan and English. He has also authored a book of poetry on the life of Guru Rinpoche entitled *Praise to the Lotus Born: A Verse Garland of Waves of Devotion*, and a unique two-volume cultural and religious history of Tibet entitled *The Six Sublime Pillars of the Nyingma School*, which details the historical bases of the dharma in Tibet from the sixth through ninth centuries. At present, this is one of the only books that conveys the dharma activities of this historical period in such depth, and was even encouraged by H.H. Dudjom Rinpoche to be completed as an important contribution to the history of the kama lineage.

Khenpo Rinpoche has also co-authored a number of books in English on dharma subjects with his brother Khenchen Palden Sherab Rinpoche, listed on the following page.

Padmasambhava Buddhist Center

Venerable Khenchen Palden Sherab Rinpoche and Venerable Khenpo Tsewang Dongyal Rinpoche have established Padmasambhava Buddhist Center to preserve in its entirety the authentic message of Buddha Shakyamuni and Guru Padmasambhava, and in particular to teach the traditions of the Nyingma School and Vajrayana Buddhism. PBC now includes over twenty centers in the U.S.A., Russia, Canada, and Puerto Rico, in addition to monastic institutions in India, Russia, and the U.S.A.

Padmasambhava Buddhist Center is dedicated to world peace and the supreme good fortune and well-being of all.

The Samye Translation Group was founded by the Venerable Khenpo Rinpoches to commemorate and preserve the great ancient tradition of translation that was firmly established during the glorious Tibetan Buddhist era of the seventh through tenth centuries. As a reflection of gratitude for the unique activities of these enlightened translators, the Samye Translation Group publishes dharma books that cover all nine-yana teachings of the Nyingma School of Tibetan Buddhism, including shedra philosophical books.

For more information about the Venerable Khenpos' activities, the Samye Translation Group, or Padmasambhava Buddhist Center, please contact:

Padma Samye Ling
618 Buddha Highway
Sidney Center, NY 13839
(607) 865-8068

www.padmasambhava.org

Other Publications by the Authors

Ceaseless Echoes of the Great Silence: A Commentary on the Heart Sutra

Prajnaparamita: The Six Perfections

Light of the Three Jewels

Lion's Gaze: A Commentary on the Tsig Sum Nedek

Door to Inconceivable Wisdom and Compassion

The Six Unique Distinctions of the Nyingma School, Volumes 1 & 2

Praise to the Lotus Born: A Verse Garland of Waves of Devotion

The Smile of Sun and Moon: A Commentary on The Praise to the Twenty-One Taras

Opening to Our Primordial Nature

Tara's Enlightened Activity

PSL Shedra Series:
> *Opening the Clear Vision of the Vaibhashika and Sautrantika Schools*
> *Opening the Clear Vision of the Mind Only School*
> *Opening the Wisdom Door of the Madhyamaka School*
> *Opening the Wisdom Door of the Rangtong & Shentong Views*
> *Opening the Wisdom Door of the Outer Tantras*

Heart Essence of Chetsun: Voice of the Lion (restricted)

Echoes of Dream Boy: Exalting the Realization of the Yogis and Yoginis

Jubilant Laughter of the Three Roots: Praise to the Inconceivable Lotus Land

Illuminating the Path: Ngondro Instructions According to the Nyingma School of Vajrayana Buddhism

Light of Fearless Indestructible Wisdom: The Life and Legacy of His Holiness Dudjom Rinpoche

More information about these and other works by the Venerable Khenpo Rinpoches, including practice texts such as the Vajrakilaya sadhana, can be found online at: www.padmasambhava.org/chiso.

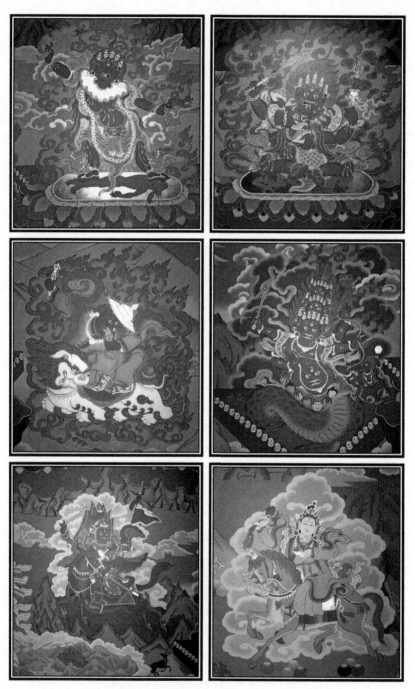

Dharma Protectors Ekajati, Mahakala, Dorje Legpa,
Rahula, Meodong, and Achi Chokyi Dolma